Utility Quilting

Simple Solutions for Quick Hand Quilting

By Carolyn Forster

Landauer Publishing, LLC

Utility Quilting
By Carolyn Forster

Copyright © 2011 by Landauer Publishing, LLC
Utility Quilting projects
Copyright © 2011 by Carolyn Forster

This book was designed, produced,
and published by Landauer Publishing, LLC
3100 101st Street, Urbandale, IA 50322
www.landauercorp.com
515/287/2144   800/557/2144

President/Publisher: Jeramy Lanigan Landauer
Vice President of Sales and Administration:
        Kitty Jacobson
Editor: Jeri Simon
Art Director: Laurel Albright
Designer, Utility Quilting: Lyne Neymeyer
Technical Illustrator: Linda Bender
Photographer: Sue Voegtlin

All rights reserved. No part of this book may
be reproduced or transmitted in any form by
any means, electronic or mechanical, including
photocopying, recording, or by any information
storage and retrieval system without permission
in writing from the publisher with the exception
that the publisher grants permission to enlarge the
template patterns in this book for personal
use only. The scanning, uploading and distribution
of this book or any part thereof, via the Internet
or any other means without permission from the
publisher is illegal and punishable by law. The
publisher presents the information in this book
in good faith. No warranty is given, nor are
results guaranteed.

ISBN 13: 978-1-935726-14-2
ISBN 10:   1-935726-14-5

Library of Congress Control Number: 2011907296
This book printed on acid-free paper.
Printed in United States

10-9-8-7-6-5-4-3-2-1

Carolyn has been making quilts since her late teens and has been teaching now for over 15 years. She has had quilt projects published in a number of books and magazines. She enjoys sharing quilt designs and projects that help make patchwork and quilting easy and accessible to everyone.

To find out more about utility quilting, or to contact Carolyn about classes, go to:
www.carolynforster.co.uk
E-mail: carolynforster@hotmail.co.uk
or write to her at:
23 Woodbury Park Road
Tunbridge Wells, Kent
TN4 9NQ, UK

Dedication
For my parents John and Jeanette Shephard, who have always supported me in my stitching.

Contents

Introduction

What is Utility Quilting?

We are all familiar with quilting, the running stitches that hold the layers of a quilt together, but we may be less familiar with the term utility quilting. Utility quilting is quilting that gets the job done.

Utility quilting can be seen on the first quilts ever made. Look at collections in museums and you will certainly see the beautifully executed stitches and ornate designs, but you will also find quilts that have simpler designs and often bigger stitches and thicker threads. The utility quilting on these quilts got the job done. Nothing more, nothing less. It is not fussy and fancy or ornate. Utility quilting is functional rather than ornamental. It can apply to the design or the stitching, and both can be combined. For the women making the quilts it allowed them to finish the job and get the quilt on the bed.

Quilts held together with basic stitching and using simple designs can be seen all over the world, from Waggas in Australia, Borromono in Japan, Kantha in Bangladesh, Amish in America and strippy quilts in northern England. Taking inspiration from our forebears and around the world, today we can hand quilt our quilts quickly and attractively.

Looking for further definitions of the word utility I found that in economics it is used to describe a measure of relative satisfaction. We can also use this definition in that sense when applied to our quilting. Many quilters still enjoy the process of hand quilting, but sometimes need it to be simpler and quicker in this modern day.

This applies well to the idea of 'utility quilting' our quilts. There is definitely a level of satisfaction to be achieved by being able to quickly and easily quilt our quilts!

Utility Quilting Designs

Utility quilting designs are often all over designs that do not necessarily relate to the pieced quilt top. They give the quilt an even amount of quilting all over.

If you look at old quilts, and even those in museum collections, although many may be beautifully and intricately quilted with feathers, wreaths, flowers and vines, you will also see many with an all over quilting design that covers the quilt or large parts of it.

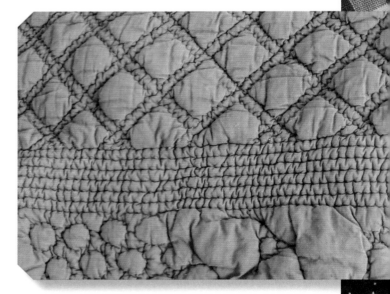

This quilt from Provencal, France, has fancy vines in the border, but the entire centre has been quilted with hanging diamonds.

Often times the quilt was quilted simply to keep the batting in place during laundering. It did not need to be fancy and time consuming since the idea was to get the quilt on a bed sooner rather than later. It is also possible that stitchers could learn or hone their quilting skills with this style of quilting, as it is easier to quilt the utility designs, rather than trying to follow intricate patterns.

Utility quilting is not fancy. It takes a minimal amount of marking. It can be quilted in one direction, so there is no twisting and turning of the quilt to maneuver it into the right position. It is often a quick way to hand quilt (or sometimes machine quilt) a top to give an even amount of quilting over all. An advantage of the all over design is it tends to act as a unifying factor, often bringing a 'oneness' to otherwise disparate fabric and piecing combinations.

This 19th century scrap quilt is quilted all over with single cross hatching. This helps to unify the design.

Well Worn Functionality

Due to the functionality of the quilts that utility stitching and quilting designs were used on, many show signs of wear and tear. But there is usually enough stitching left to see how these designs made quilting the quilt a quick and easy process.

This vintage quilt shows very apparent signs of wear. It is very soft and has obviously been used and washed many times. The all over quilting design has kept the layers together, but nothing has been able to stop the fabrics from wearing thin and exposing the batting.

Utility Quilting Stitches

Utility quilting means bigger stitches and thicker thread. Larger stitches get the job done quickly and in a bold fashion. Thicker thread can also be used on its own or with the addition of buttons or felt to tie the quilt layers together.

It has been said that the use of the thicker thread came from women pulling the stitches out of grain sacks and keeping the thread to tie or quilt their quilts.

For inspiration, look at old quilts in books or museums. There will often be one or two in a collection that have been stitched with larger stitches or tied. These quilts were put together quickly and long hours were not spent on the quilting, as these quilts needed to be in use on beds. This also means that examples are not seen often as these quilts were made to be used and often wore out.

Other influences for this type of quilting is Sashiko from Japan and the Kantha work found in Bangladesh and in West Bengal, India. Examples of this work would be seen at exhibitions and trade vessels would sometimes bring back pieces of cloth with the stitching on it. All these things played a part in influencing the quilter.

*Sample of
Sashiko work,
Waves design*

Sample of Kantha work, Bangladesh

Combining the Two

When big stitches and utility quilting designs are combined, our quilts can be quilted even faster!

This is an ideal solution for the modern quilter who wants the satisfaction of hand work, but needs a speedy solution.

How does this work for us today?

Today we have many of the same reasons to want to get a quilt finished and on the bed as women 100 years ago did. In fact, we may have a lot more!

- Today, the piecing is speedy, the cutting is speedy and so the quilting process needs to be speedy as well. People still want to hand quilt. They enjoy the communal nature and the therapeutic pleasure. They like the portability….utility designs and utility stitches can speed up hand quilting for us.

- Fabrics today have bigger bolder designs. The quilts made from these fabrics are often made from big pieces. Bigger stitches and thicker threads make the design stand out and fill the space. Fine hand quilting is often 'lost' on such quilts.

- Charity quilts are often quickly sewn and need quick quilting to send them on their way to a new home. Utility methods allow for quickly made quilts to be completed.

- There are numerous new lines of fabric released each year. We want to use them all in our quilt tops and having a quick way to complete the quilting process gives us the satisfaction of a finished project, not another unfinished top.

- It is easier to learn to quilt on straight forward designs, rather than intricate ones. Utility designs tend to be easier to quilt as they can be worked in one direction, with no frequent change of direction. This allows you to build up a gentle rhythm with your work and helps you develop even stitches, which with practice will become smaller.

- Quilters often complain, 'My stitches are too big'! Well, for big stitch quilting they need to be bigger so make the most of it.

- This 'primitive-style' quilting easily lends itself to the bold contemporary fabrics and colored threads that are available.

- With quilters using a varied selection of fabrics such as linen, toile and wools, utility quilting is a forgiving style of design and stitch. It allows the fabrics to relax and move a little without restricting their natural characteristics. It is also easier to make bigger stitches on thicker fabrics instead of trying to manipulate the needle into making smaller stitches uncomfortably.

Can you 'utility quilt' on your sewing machine?

We cannot ignore the fact that as soon as our great-grandmothers had access to a sewing machine they used it to their advantage. It must have been tremendously liberating to be able to push the quilt through the throat plate, and see the layers quilted together far quicker than the women had ever done by hand.

There is no reason for you not to sew some of the designs with the sewing machine. Obvious designs would be to quilt in straight lines. Take this idea further and use a 'three step zigzag' to quilt the lines while adding a bit of movement. Less obvious choices are to use single motif embroidery stitches to 'tie' your quilt, or use a button stitching facility to sew the buttons on.

Not all the designs are suited for a domestic sewing machine. Work out which designs will be easy for you to stitch with your sewing machine. Remember, utility quilting is all about making it easy and therefore quick to do.

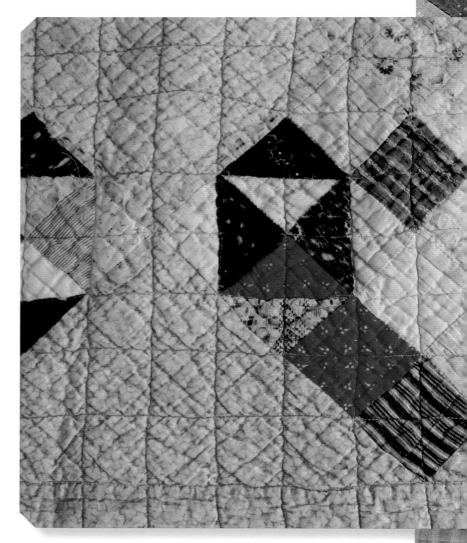

This piece of old quilt shows how the maker machine quilted in a straight grid as an all over design. She has used the grid created by the piecing to guide her.

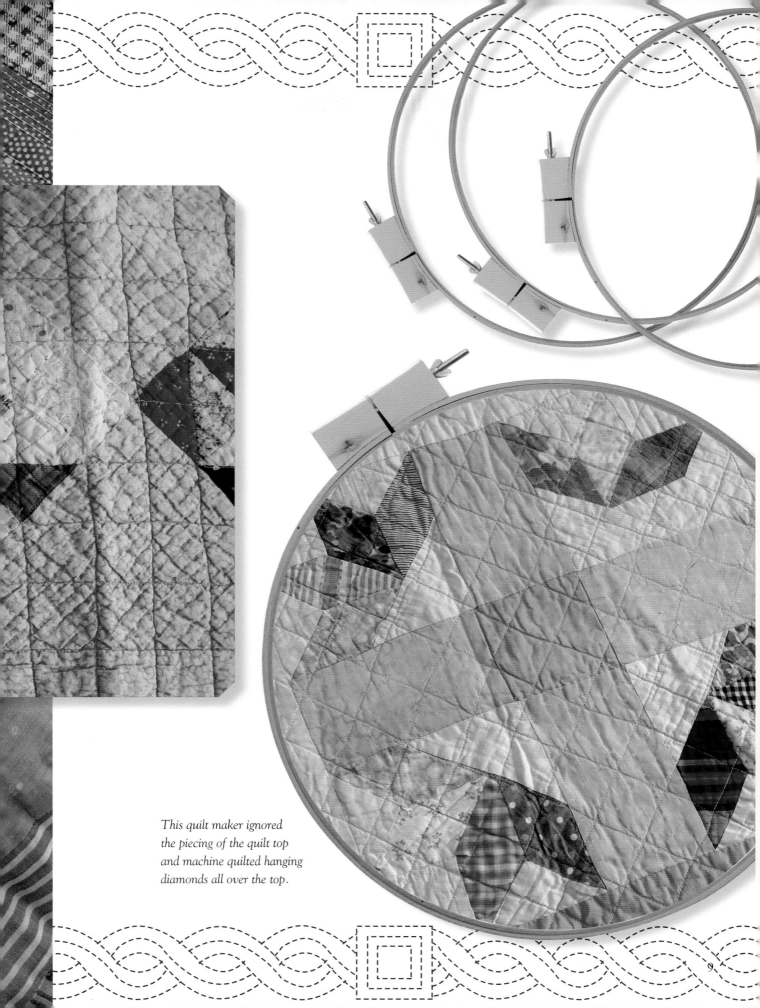

This quilt maker ignored
the piecing of the quilt top
and machine quilted hanging
diamonds all over the top.

Getting Started– Supplies

Becoming familiar with the products needed to successfully complete a quilt is as important as the quilting design and stitching.

Preparing to Quilt Supplies

There are several things to consider as you prepare your quilt for stitching. What kind of batting should I use? Should I use batting? Do I want to hand tack or safety pin baste the quilt layers together? Try different types of batting and styles of basting to determine what works best for each of your projects.

Batting

Batting is the middle layer of the quilt. There are many different brands of batting and each has its own recommendations for the amount of quilting that should be done on them.

If a batting requires quilting every 2" to 4", we can assume more time will be spent on the quilting than one requiring quilting every 10". To get the job done quickly, choose the batting that needs less quilting. Read the information on the batting packages before making your choice.

For a quickly quilted project I prefer Hobbs Heirloom® 80/20 batting. It only needs quilting every 4" so works well for Big Stitch quilting.
If I am tying a quilt I use Warm and Natural® batting. It only requires quilting every 10".

Iron on Batting

For wallhangings, table runners, or other small projects, try one of the many iron on battings that are available. These

Preparing the Quilt Layers

- Prepare your quilt top and backing fabric by pressing it. Drape them over a spare bed or stair rail to keep them from needing a second pressing.

- Unfold the batting a day before using it to allow it to relax and let any creases fall out. Leaving the batting in a steamy bathroom overnight also works well. You can also put the batting in the dryer on the refresh cycle if you are in a hurry.

Preparing to Quilt Supplies

A range of tools that can be used for preparing your quilt for quilting are shown.

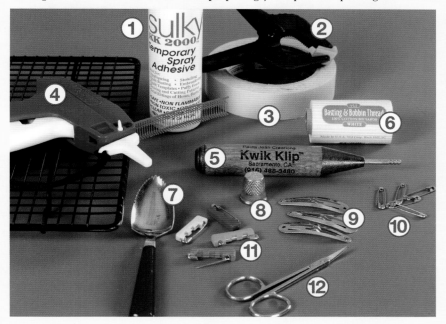

1. Spray Adhesive
2. Table Clamps
3. Masking Tape
4. Basting Gun & Grid
5. Kwik Klip™
6. Basting Thread
7. Grapefruit Spoon
8. Thimble
9. Hemming Clips
10. Safety Pins
11. Safety Pin Covers
12. Curved Scissors

battings will not 'gum up' your needle and work when hand or machine stitching. Use it on smaller projects first, then move to a larger quilt if you like the way it works. As always, follow the manufacturer's instructions for use.

Polar Fleece and Minky

Polar Fleece, Minky or Snuggle fabrics work well as quick quilt backs. They can easily be used for quilts that are 'turned through' and don't need binding. Choosing these fabrics will also eliminate the need for batting. It acts as the backing and the insulating lining. Because it is woven or knitted it will not pull apart during wear and laundering. It will also need less quilting.

Flannel sheets

Flannel sheets or sheeting by the yard can be used as batting for your quilt.

These do not need to be new, but ones that have worn out in places. Since there is no loft, bold designs with thick thread will stand out. Tying is also an option. This is a good choice for a summer quilt or table topper when you want to add a bit of weight, but no loft.

Blankets

Old blankets act as a good insulating lining, but due to their weight and thickness do not encourage excessive quilting. Tying works well, as does the addition of buttons and felt. Blankets are a good choice for flannel quilts adding extra weight and drape.

Tacking and Basting

There are several ways to prepare your quilt layers for quilting. Some people prefer hand tacking while others use the safety pin basting method. Both of

these methods are shown in Preparing to Quilt on page 16. Two alternative methods are mentioned here.

Tacking or Basting Gun

A tacking or basting gun is a quick way to baste your quilt layers before quilting. This tool resembles the gun that attaches price tags to clothing. I recommend testing on scraps of leftover fabric before using on your quilt layers. Be sure to follow manufacturer's instructions carefully if choosing this method of basting.

Spray Adhesives

Quilt layers may also be held together with spray adhesives, such as 505 Spray and Fix. It is odorless and will hold the layers together while you quilt. Follow the product instructions and work on the quilt in sections.

Marking Supplies

There are ways to cut down on the time spent marking the quilt designs on the quilt top. By keeping the marking process as simple as possible, less time is taken and you can get to the quilting more quickly.

Hera marker - One of the most traditional ways of marking a quilt is to crease or score the design into the fabric with a fine blunt instrument. The Hera is a traditional Japanese tool used for marking designs onto cloth. They were once made from bone, but today are made from plastic and will not wear out.

Soap - Dried slivers of soap can be used to mark your designs. The thin edges of the soap can be used to make lines on the quilt top. The lines can be quilted and left. They will wash away when the quilt is washed.

Chalk - Tailor's Chalk or chalk markers will give you a clear line to follow when quilting. Chalk markers come in an assortment of colors and the line brushes away as you quilt.

Masking tape - Masking tape comes in a variety of widths and is ideal for marking straight lines. Never leave the masking tape on the work when you are not stitching. Exposure to heat or sunlight can be detrimental to the glues and make them harder to remove from the fabric.

Water-soluble or artist's pencils - These pencils can be used if you treat the area you are marking with spray starch before you begin. Water-soluble markers will need water to wash away the mark. Keep them sharp for a fine line.

Spray Starch – Many quilters use spray starch when they piece their tops, so marking the designs with a water soluble or artist's pencil which brushes off is a good choice.

Freezer Paper or Contact Paper – Make your design templates from freezer paper or adhesive-backed contact paper. This way you will not need to transfer the shape, just adhere it to the quilt top and quilt around it. Peel the template away when you are done and reapply the shape as needed. These templates will generally last through more than one application.

Paper – Regular copy paper can be used to create templates. Draw the template on the paper and make copies. Cut out and apply 202™ temporary adhesive or 404™ permanent repositionable adhesive to the back. Adhere the template to the quilt top and quilt around it. Peel the template away when you are done and reapply the shape as needed to continue the design.

Tip
When you remove the masking tape strips roll them into a ball with the sticky side on the outside. Use it to pick stray threads off of your work.

Marking the Designs Supplies

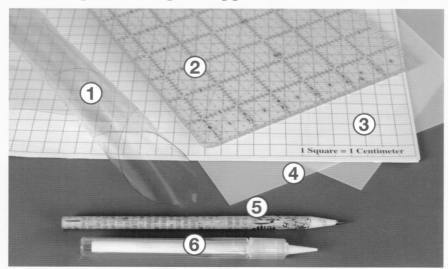

These are a few of the tools that can be used for marking a design on the quilt top. Experiment until you find the tools you prefer.

1. Upholstery Vinyl
2. Acrylic Ruler
3. Grid Paper
4. Template Plastic
5. Artist's Pencil
6. Chalk Marker

Binding Supplies

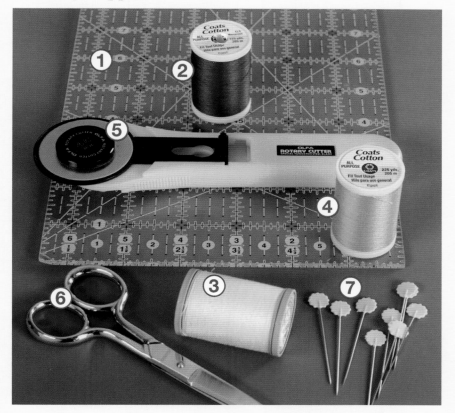

1. Acrylic Ruler
2.-4. Thread to Match Your Project
5. Rotary Cutter
6. Scissors
7. Pins

Binding Supplies

Binding adds strength and another opportunity for stitching to your quilt. I have provided you with four techniques for finishing your quilt beginning on page 70. Choose the style of binding that suits your project and time frame.

Stitching Supplies

When it comes to stitching the design on your quilt top, the main tools needed will be needle and thread. Experiment with a variety of threads when tying or stitching your design. Each will give your quilt a unique look.

Thread

Threads used for Big Stitch and utility quilting are generally thicker than regular quilting thread. There is a wide selection of threads to choose from and your decision may vary with each project depending on the look you want.

Keep a variety of threads on hand to make your piecing and quilting go more quickly. I generally have eight large spools of thread in colors that will match or complement any project I am working on. You do not actually have to have the same color thread as your fabric, just one that acts as a 'shadow'. The color will sink into the background and disappear.

The thread colors I always have on hand include: cream, dark cream, light gray, dark gray, tan, black, navy and Coats 5013.

With practice you will find your own favorite thread colors. Buy the biggest spool you can and wind three or four bobbins at a time to save time and effort later.

Tip

A great time saver for piecing is to buy ready wound bobbins. This way you will always have one ready to be dropped into the sewing machine.

Stitching Supplies

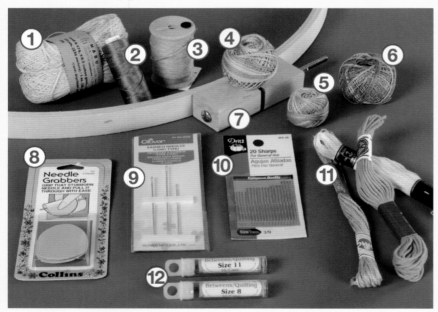

1. Yarn
2.-6. Thread to Match Your Project
7. Hoop
8. Needle Grabber
9. Sashiko Needles
10. Variety of Sharps
11. Floss to Match Your Project
12. Selection of Betweens

Needles

Needles used for Big Stitch and utility quilting will vary depending on the thread used. This is necessary in order to accommodate the thickness of thread and to enable you to make longer stitches more comfortably.

Have a selection of needles on hand to give you the most flexibility with your quilting. Remember, there is no real rule. You are just trying to find a needle size that is comfortable for you.

Some needle suggestions for Big Stitch and tying include: Betweens sizes 3 and 5, Chenille sizes 22 and 24, Sharps sizes 3 and 5 and Sashiko. For fine hand quilting try Betweens sizes 8 to 11.

Threads

A selection of threads is shown, but experiment to see what looks best on each of your quilts.

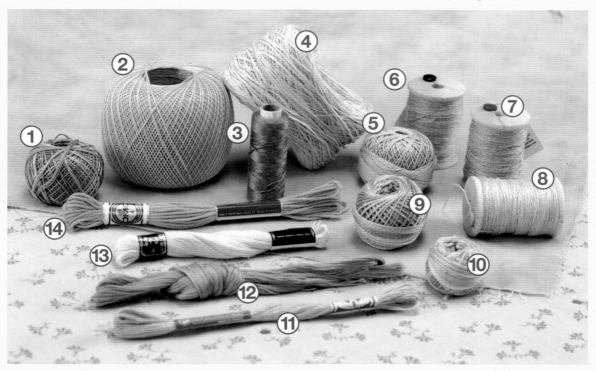

1. Valdani Variegated Pearl Cotton 12
2. Crochet Cotton 20
3. Needleworks/Quilts Cosmo multi work
4. Habu Japanese Yarn
5. Valdani Pearl Cotton 12
6. Hillcreek Designs Normandy Linen 40/2
7. Hillcreek Designs Normandy Linen 30/3
8. Hillcreek Designs Normandy Linen 16/2
9. Valdani Pearl Cotton 5
10. Valdani 3-strand Floss
11. DMC Linen Embroidery Floss
12. Valdani Variegated 3-strand Floss
13. Anchor Cotton A Broder 16
14. DMC Cotton Tapisserie 4

Preparing to Quilt

Refer to Getting Started, Preparing to Quilt Supplies on page 10 before beginning.
With a little preparation and thought, the process of layering and basting your quilt can be sped up. Determine how you plan to quilt your quilt and then work out the best tacking or basting method before you begin.

Things to Consider Before You Start

- Prepare your quilt top and backing fabric by pressing it. Drape both over a spare bed or stair rail to keep them from needing a second pressing.

- Unfold the batting a day before using it to allow it to relax and let any creases fall out. Leaving the batting in a steamy bathroom overnight also works well. You can also put the batting in the dryer on the refresh cycle if you are in a hurry.

- Think about how you are going to quilt your quilt before you baste it. Depending on the method you use, you may not need to baste the layers together.

- Traditional stand-up frames with rollers eliminate the basting process completely. This is a good option if you have the space at home and enjoy hand quilting. These frames are not easy to shift from one room to another so make sure you place it in your favorite quilting spot.

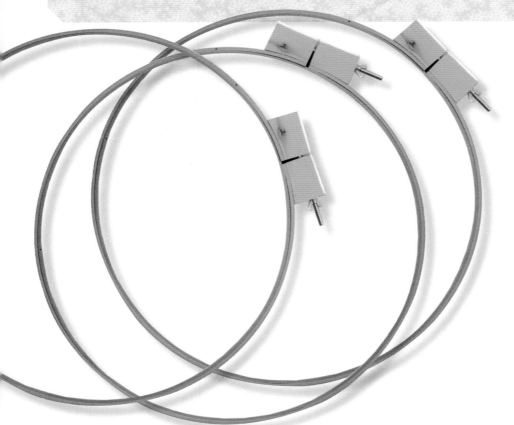

Circular hoops work well when hand tacking is used. Safety pins tend to get in the way of the hoop and often need to be taken out when you reposition the hoop on your quilt. It is important to be aware of this before you start.

Tip
When you have finished quilting, remember to take your work out of the hoop, so the quilt will not distort over time.

Lap quilting does not offer the additional stability a hoop gives the work, so denser basting is needed to stop the layers from shifting. Baste every 4" rather than the usual 6". Use your closed fist as a gauge between basting stitches rather than a spread hand.

Hand Tacking or Basting the Quilt Layers Together

Everyone has different reasons for wanting the basting stage to be done quickly. Many find it the most tedious part of the quilt making process. However, it is also one of the most important, since it holds the layers of the quilt together securely for quilting.

Try different hand tacking and basting techniques to find one that suits your time frame and circumstances. You will find that each project will dictate the type of basting technique you use.

Generally, the tacking or basting stitches should form a grid. The grid is often dictated by the patches in the quilt. The gap between basting lines should be no larger than 6". If the patchwork does not have a grid to follow, use your hand span as a guide.

Hand Tacking

Hand tacking or basting a quilt gives you the best control over the quilt layers and does not add any extra weight or bulk.

One of the reasons I like to hand baste is it gives me time to look at the quilt and determine how it might best be quilted. When I am piecing a quilt I do not always think about how it will be quilted. The basting process gives me that time.

How to Hand Tack

A Sharps size 6 needle and tacking thread are my favorite tools when hand tacking my quilt layers together.

When hand basting a quilt, start with a backstitch and a knot.

Work the stitches from right to left on the quilt. The stitches will be about a half-inch long and evenly spaced. Remember to form a grid while tacking.
Note: Work left to right if you are left handed.

Hand Tacking continued

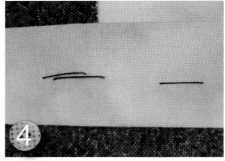

Finish with a backstitch to keep the thread secure.

To help ease the needle up through the layers use a teaspoon or grapefruit spoon. As the needle and your hands are always on the top of the quilt, your fingers can get sore as the needle pushes up against them. Pushing the needle up against the edge of a grapefruit spoon makes the process quicker.

Tips for hand tacking

- Use a floor at a community center or church. Book the space when you know the cleaner has just been there. This saves you from moving your own furniture around to make room for the quilt on the floor.

- Use their large tables if kneeling on the floor is not an option.

- Use a kneeling mat or knee pads for any tacking done on the floor.

- Use a carpeted floor to prevent the quilt from shifting. The edges can be secured with masking tape

- Baste a quilt with a group of friends.

- If a group near you has a frame for basting, check to see if they offer a quilt basting service.

- Many long arm quilters offer a basting service. This thread-basted method offers all the advantages of manageability and no added weight.

- Learn to tabletop baste. Invest in sturdy collapsible tables for basting at home.

Tip

I use tacking thread when basting my quilt layers together. It is less expensive than regular thread and comes on big spools. It breaks easily when snapped between my fingers, but holds my quilt layers securely together for quilting. Coats & Clark and Gutterman are two of the tacking threads I use. I also like to use a Sharps needle size 6.

Tailor's Basting

Some people find the action of tacking uncomfortable, as the needle is held horizontal to your body. If this is the case for you, try Tailor's Basting. The needle is held so it points at your body, which is sometimes a more natural action.

When using this stitch tack the quilt in rows 6" apart. Unlike a straight basting stitch, you will not need to create a grid.

TOOLS TO
MAKE IT
QUICKER

Thimble
Spoon
Masking tape
Needles
Kneeling mat
Knee pads

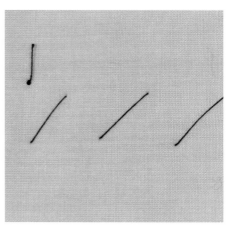

Thread the needle with tacking thread and knot the end. Work the stitch from right to left on the quilt. **Note:** Work left to right if you are left handed.

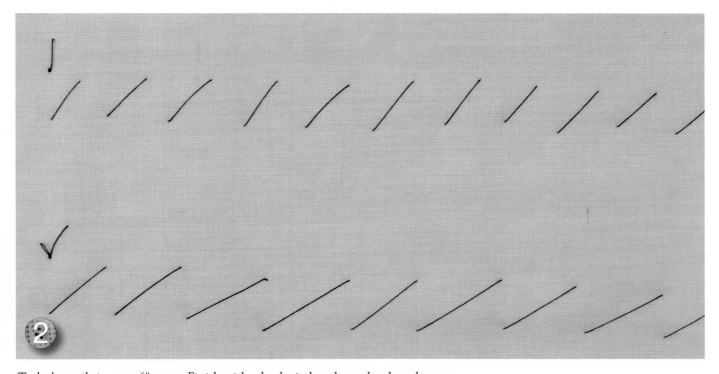

Tack the quilt in rows 6" apart. Finish with a backstitch to keep the thread secure.

Assembling the Quilt Layers for Basting

The three layers of your quilt–backing, batting and top–need to be smooth and free of wrinkles before the basting process can be done. Basting will keep the layers securely together for quilting.

Press the backing fabric and lay it on the floor wrong side up. Smooth it out flat, securing it to the floor with masking tape at the corners and mid-points on all four sides.

Note: DO NOT stretch the fabric. If you stretch the fabric, it will retract back to its natural place when the masking tape comes off after basting. This will cause puckers in your quilt back.

Fold the batting into quarters. Line up the outside edge of the batting with the corner of the backing fabric and unfold a quarter at a time, smoothing the batting over the backing fabric. The middle of the backing and batting should now be centered.

Press the quilt top and place it on top of the batting, right side up. You may also fold the quilt top into quarters, as was done with the batting. Leave approximately 2½" of batting showing around the edge of the quilt top. Smooth out the quilt top until it is flat and free of wrinkles. Add squares of masking tape at the corners.

Safety pin the three layers together in the center, at the corners and at the mid-point of each side. This keeps things in place while basting.

Basting the layers together

When basting a quilt I find it easier to tack in a grid system. If I always use the same system, then I don't have to think or plan, just baste!

I baste the quilts on a carpeted floor. This helps keep the layers from shifting.

Note: If you are finishing your quilt by tying the layers together, you may be able to eliminate the basting process. See Knots and Tying on page 62.

Tip

If you have hardwood or linoleum floors, they may need protection from the needle. Protect the floor by using a rotary cutting mat between the backing and the floor and move the mat as you baste. You can also tabletop baste your quilts.

This quilt was tied at the corners of the pieced blocks and equal intervals in the sashing. If you are tying your quilt layers, you may not need to hand tack or baste.

System One

This is the system I use when I hand baste my quilts on the floor. It smooths out any wrinkles that may arise.

Lay out the quilt layers following the directions in Assembling the Quilt Layers for Basting.

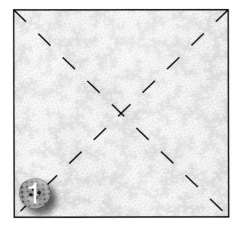

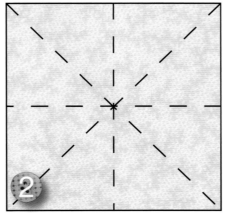

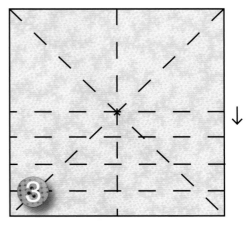

Using the tacking thread and beginning with a knot and a backstitch, baste the diagonal lines. Finish with a backstitch.

Baste across the middle in both directions. Take out pins as you come to them.

Using your hand span as a guide, baste in rows beginning in the center and working toward the outer edge. When this section is full, move to the next.

Note: Use a grapefruit spoon or wear a thimble when bringing the needle up out of the quilt. You are working from the top of the quilt at all times. You should never have your hand under the quilt as this could disturb the layers or cause them to shift.

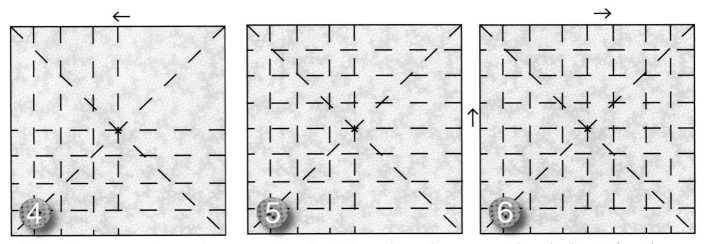

There are four sections to baste in the same manner as Step 3. Remember to always start your line of tacking in the quilt center and work toward the outer edge.

When the grid is complete, baste $\frac{1}{4}$" from the outside edge of the quilt layers. This will stop the edges from fraying or stretching before quilting. The stitches will be removed as you quilt.

Remove the masking tape from the edges of your quilt layers. You can now fold the extra batting and backing fabric over and tack it, abutting it with the edge of the quilt.

System Two

This system allows the quilt to be evenly basted in smaller sections.

Lay out the quilt layers following the directions in Assembling the Quilt Layers for Basting.

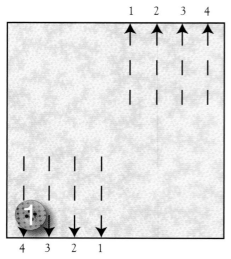

Baste the first two sections in vertical rows as shown, beginning in the center and working toward the outer edge. Take out pins as you come to them.

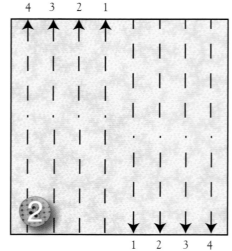

Continue with the next two sections.

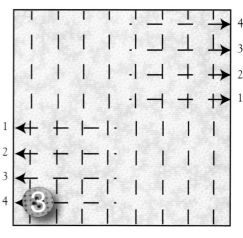

Return to the first two sections and baste in horizontal rows as shown.

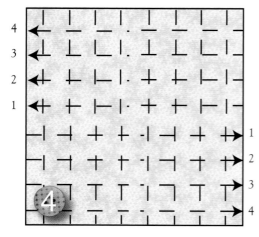

Baste the final two sections in horizontal rows.

When the grid is complete, baste ¼" from the outside edge of the quilt layers. This will stop the edges from fraying or stretching before quilting. The stitches will be removed as you quilt.

Remove the masking tape from the edges of your quilt layers. You can now fold the extra batting and backing fabric over and tack it, abutting it with the edge of the quilt.

System Three

This system works from the center outward like the rays of the sun. It has the appearance of a radial, less rigid grid.

Lay out the quilt layers following the directions in Assembling the Quilt Layers for Basting.

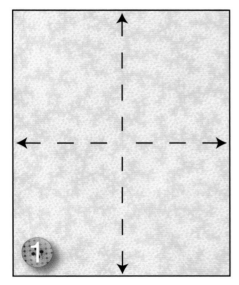

Baste the center lines, beginning in the middle of the quilt layers and working toward the outer edge. Take out pins as you come to them.

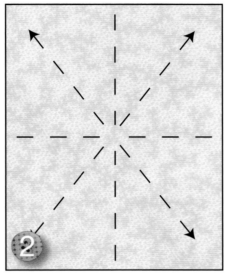

Baste diagonal lines between the center lines, as shown.

When the grid is complete, baste ¼" from the outside edge of the quilt layers. This will stop the edges from fraying or stretching before quilting. The stitches will be removed as you quilt.

Remove the masking tape from the edges of your quilt layers. You can now fold the extra batting and backing fabric over and tack it, abutting it with the edge of the quilt.

Continue basting diagonal lines in the same manner until the quilt layers are secure.

Tabletop Basting

If you are unable to baste or hand tack your quilt on the floor, try tabletop basting. You can baste a large quilt on a table using clips or clamps to hold it in place.

Things You Will Need for Tabletop Basting

- A table at a comfortable height for you.
  Note: If the table is not high enough, invest in plastic piping that will fit on the bottom of the legs, increasing the height, or purchase table risers.

- I use an adjustable office chair so I can sit to baste.

- Masking tape, toothpicks or skewers.

- Clips, clamps or Bulldog clips.

- Sharps size 6 needle or needle of your choice (if hand basting).

- Basting or other thread (if hand basting).

- Safety pins (if pin basting).

Mark the center of the table, vertically and horizontally, with a toothpick, skewer or other thin object. Keep in place with masking tape.
Note: I do this so I can feel the center of the table through the quilt layers. You may also place masking tape at the mid-point of each side of the table.

Press the backing fabric and fold into quarters, wrong sides together. Place the folded backing fabric on the table, right side up, matching the center of the fabric with the center of the table.

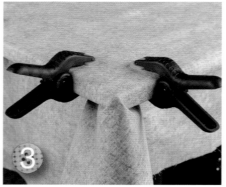

Unfold the fabric. Line up the edges with the marked points on the sides of the table to keep it straight. Use clips to secure the fabric to the edges of the table.
Note: If the quilt is smaller than the table, tape the edges that don't hang over in place.

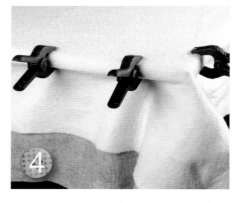

Fold the batting in the same way and place it on top of the backing fabric matching the center points. Smooth the batting over the backing fabric. Do not stretch it. Clip into place using the same clips as for the backing.

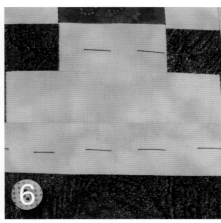

Press the quilt top and fold into quarters, right sides together. Place the quilt top on the batting matching the center points. Smooth out any creases as you unfold the quilt top. Use the clips to hold the three layers together.

Baste the area secured on the table. Work from right to left, basting in rows approximately 6" apart.
Note: Baste left to right if you are left handed.

When the first area is complete remove the clips and masking tape. Shift the layers away from you so the next unbasted area is on the tabletop. Secure the side of the quilt that has been basted with clips or masking tape. Pull the backing taut and secure the next unbasted section with clips to the opposite side of the tabletop. Baste as before.

Continue this process until the entire quilt has been basted. You may need to move the quilt several times to completely baste it.

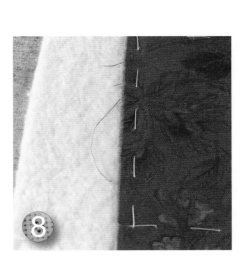

When finished, tack ¼" around the outside edge of the quilt top.

Other Tacking and Basting Options

If hand tacking a quilt comfortably and quickly is not an option for you, consider one of the alternative techniques listed here. For maximum efficiency, combine any of the following techniques with tabletop basting.

TOOLS TO MAKE IT QUICKER

1" safety pins (open)

Safety pin covers

Kwik Klip® or grapefruit spoon

Safety Pin Basting

When basting with safety pins, they should be placed approximately every 6" to 8". Test this with the span of your hand. If your hand is spread out on the quilt top and you are not touching safety pins, add a few more.

Use a Kwik Klip® or grapefruit spoon to close the safety pins. Plastic covers are also available for safety pins giving your fingers something larger to grip. All three of these tools will help you avoid sore fingers.

Layer the backing, batting and quilt top following steps 1–5 in Tabletop Basting.

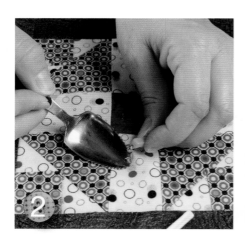

Beginning at the center and working from the top of the quilt, insert the safety pin and bring it back up through all three layers. Bring the point of the safety pin up against the edge of the grapefruit spoon or Kwik Klip® and clip it closed.

Continue to pin baste your quilt layers. Do a hand span check every once in a while to make sure you are spacing the safety pins correctly. The pins should not be too densely or sparsely placed. If you can spread your hand on the quilt and touch pins, that is a good density.

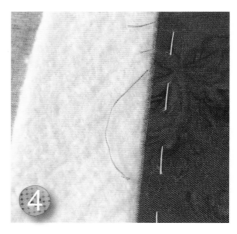

When the quilt is covered with pins, tack ¼" around the outside edge of the quilt top.

Spray Adhesives

Quilt layers may also be held together with spray adhesives, such as 505 Spray and Fix or Sulky® Temporary Spray Adhesive. It is odorless and will hold the layers together while you quilt. Follow the product instructions and work on the quilt in sections.

Tacking or Basting Gun

A tacking or basting gun is a quick way to baste your quilt layers before quilting. This tool resembles the gun that attaches price tags to clothing. I recommend testing on scraps of leftover fabric before using on your quilt layers. Be sure to follow manufacturer's instructions carefully if choosing this method of basting.

When preparing your quilt layers for stitching, consider the design you will be using. The quilt above was machine stitched in a straight grid. The quilt at left was hand quilted with an elbow quilting design. See page 36.

27

Utility Quilting Designs

Historically quilts were often stitched out of necessity. Utility quilting designs were used because they required minimal marking and were quick to quilt compared to elaborate feathers and wreaths. The stitch pattern was repeated and sewn all over the quilt top without taking the pieced patchwork into account.

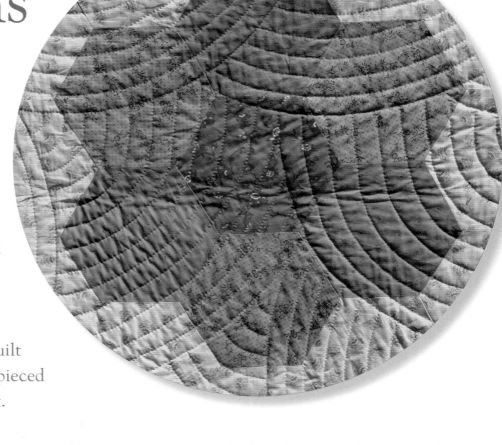

The quilting designs were created from items commonly found in most homes, such as cups, plates and even one's elbow. A straight edge was often made by coating a piece of string with flour.

Refer to Getting Started, Marking the Designs supplies on page 12 before beginning.

Big Stitch Quilting

You can use big stitches or the small stitches used in fine hand quilting with the utility designs on the following pages. If you use big stitches, space your designs accordingly—remember, bigger spaces and bolder patterns. Practice with the stitches beginning on page 52 to determine which ones you prefer with each quilting design.

Fine Hand Quilting

If you are planning to use fine hand quilting stitches, the designs will still work up quickly, but you will be using regular quilting thread and a small quilting needle. I suggest you buy a variety pack of Betweens quilting needles. Start with the smallest needle with which you feel comfortable. After some practice you should be sewing with a size 10 or 11 needle. The thought is—the smaller the needle, the smaller your stitches. Some hand quilters prefer a longer needle. This is a matter of preference and there is no right or wrong.

Machine Quilting

Many of the utility quilting designs shown can be stitched on the sewing machine. Use your favorite machine quilting thread and a free motion foot, or even a walking foot, to stitch the designs. Practice to get the results you want.

Tip
With Betweens needles, the larger the number the smaller the needle.

Auditioning the designs

It is often hard to know what a design will look like when it is quilted. While you can draw it on paper to see the scale and repeat, you really need to see it on the quilt before you start. You can audition the design without actually marking on your quilt. This way if the design does not work out it can be changed.

 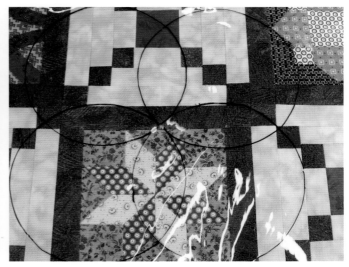

Upholstery vinyl is a great tool for auditioning a quilting design on the quilt top. It is a clear, inexpensive plastic that can be purchased from any store that has an upholstery fabric department. Lay the clear vinyl over the quilt top and use a washable felt tip pen to draw your design on the quilt. If you need to alter the design, wipe the marks off and begin again.

Amish Wave/Mennonite Fan Design

The fan design was so easy to execute that many individuals and church groups used it in their work. Therefore it became known by as many different names as the people who used it. Some of these design names include Amish Wave, Mennonite Fan, Baptist Fan and Wave.

The fan design is popular because...

- It is quilted on the bias which makes it easier to quilt.

- The design covers the entire quilt, ignoring the piecing and acting as a unifying feature.

- It can be stitched by any level of quilter.

- It can be quilted by groups around a frame working from the outside edge toward the quilt center.

- The fan design is often seen with single lines of quilting, but can also be worked with two or three lines of quilting.

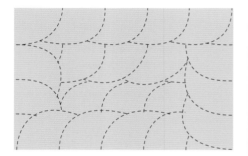

Fan shaped designs, such as the Amish Wave or Mennonite Fan, are quilted from the outside edge of the quilt and worked in toward the center. It can also be stitched in rows from bottom to top.

If a quilt was being quilted in a square frame by a group of women, one could sit on each side and quilt the design working in toward the quilt's center.

 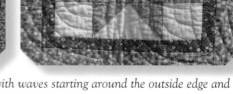

The Stars sampler quilt, above, is quilted with waves starting around the outside edge and working in toward the quilt center.

The fan design on this antique quilt covers the quilt but ignores the piecing. There is approximately a thumb width between the lines of quilting.

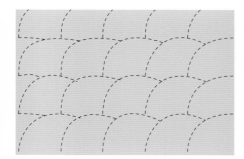

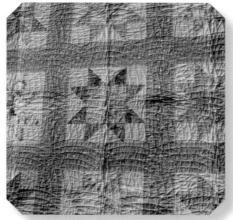

If you are quilting the fan design on a frame with rollers, you will quilt the design in rows.

Start at the bottom of the quilt and work toward the top, rolling the quilt as you go.

The Star sampler quilt, above, is quilted from the bottom upward using the Amish Wave design.

Fan quilting is used on the Star quilt, above, to unify the patchwork and give an even, all over quilting to the quilt.

Making a Fan Design Template

To create the fan design on your quilt top, a template can be used. You can make your own template in any size by using a compass or round household item.

Using a Compass

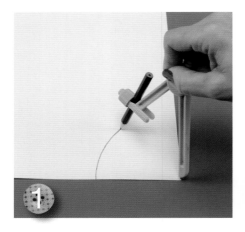

1 Set the compass to the arc size you desire. Place the compass in the corner of a sheet of paper and draw a quarter circle.

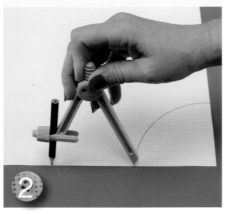

2 Move the compass to the point where the beginning quarter circle line touched the edge of the paper.

3 Draw another arc until it reaches the first arc.

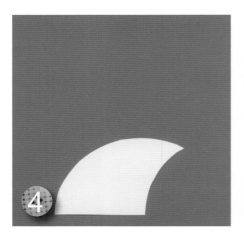

4 Cut out the second arc.

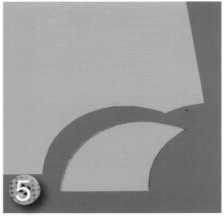

5 Trace your template design onto template plastic and cut out.

Using a Round Object

1 Using a pencil and piece of paper, trace around a plate or other round object.

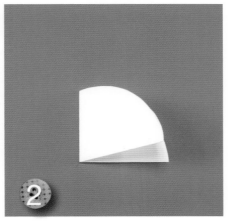

2 Cut out the traced circle and fold it into quarters.

3 Use this quarter to draw the first arc onto template plastic.

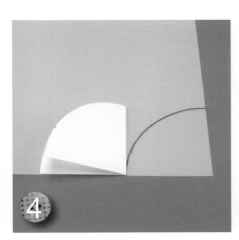

4 Keeping the paper folded, line up the straight folded edge with the curve of the first drawn arc.

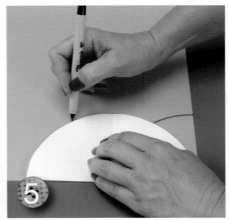

5 Unfold the quarter to make a half circle and draw around this shape until the line of the second arc meets the line of the first. Remove the paper circle.

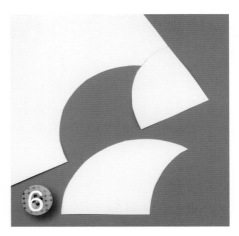

6 Cut out the second drawn shape. This is the template for your fan quilting.

Marking the Fan Design

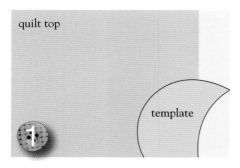

1 Place the fan template in the bottom right hand corner of the quilt, matching the straight edges. Draw around the arc of the template.
Note: Begin in the left hand corner if you are left handed.

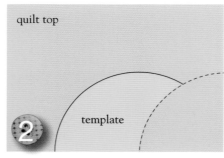

2 Place the inner curve of the template against the outer curve of the first marked arc. Draw around the outer template curve.

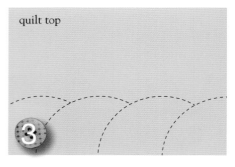

3 Continue marking the bottom row of designs in this manner. When you come to the edge of the quilt, the design will run off the edge.

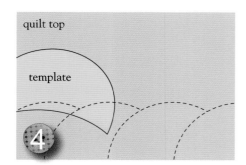

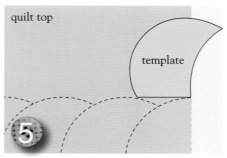

4 **5** Position the template to turn the corner to begin the next row. If you prefer, you may move the template and mark the next row directly above the first.

When you quilt the fan design, the marked outer arc will be quilted top to bottom. The unmarked inner arcs will be quilted the distance of the needle length or the width of your thumb knuckle. If you prefer you may mark the inner curves with dashed lines before quilting.
Note: The large marked arcs can contain varying numbers of smaller arcs. This is up to the individual quilter.

Fan Quilting Variations

Thumb or Egg Cup Quilting

Thumb or egg cup quilting is worked from the smallest curve out toward the largest. All the fans should have the same number of curves, but may be slightly different sizes depending on the accuracy of the quilter.

Marking the Thumb/Egg Cup Design

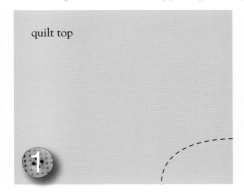

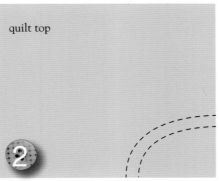

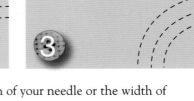

Begin by using your thumb to determine the size of the first curve. Mark around the curve.
Note: You may also use a small, circular household object such as an egg cup.

Mark the larger curves using the length of your needle or the width of your thumb to determine distance between lines. These arcs can be drawn freehand.

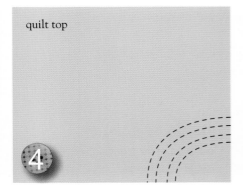

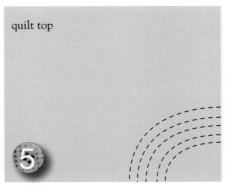

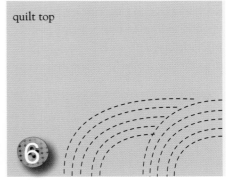

Stop marking when the fan design is the desired size. Begin marking the next fan, remembering to draw the same number of curves as the first fan. The subsequent sizes of your curves may vary slightly from those of the first fan.

When you quilt, the marked inner arc of the fan design will be quilted first. Work your way out toward the larger arcs.

Elbow Quilting

Elbow quilting differs from the general fan design because the first large arc is marked by using your elbow as the pivot point. For this reason you do not need a template. You can usually tell if the design is elbow quilted since the size of the first arc is generally larger than if a template had been used. The distance between the inner lines are determined by using the length of your needle or the width of your thumb. These fans are quilted beginning with the large curve and working toward the smallest.

Hexagon quilt, 2010
Pieced and quilted by Carolyn Forster
Due to the large size of the hexagons (8" across)
the scale of the elbow quilting fits perfectly
with the piecing.

Teacup/Wine Glass/Pumpkin Seed Design

The teacup design looks complicated but is deceptively simple. It is commonly named after the household item used to make the circles, hence teacup and wine glass. To make larger circles, simply use a larger round household item as your starting point. For example, a saucepan lid could be used.

Marking the quilt with overlapping circles across the quilt creates seedlike shapes which create a design referred to as Pumpkin Seed. Although you draw individual circles the design is quilted in wavy lines.

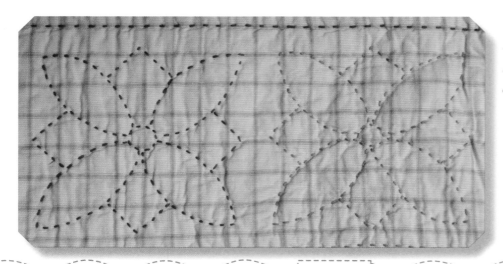

The quilt, at left, uses a variation of the pumpkin seed design in the border.

Making a Circle Template

Use this method to make your circle template when the size does not have to be too precise. Find a round item similar to the size template you need. For example, use teacups or glasses for smaller circles and plates or saucepan lids for larger ones.

Using a Round Object

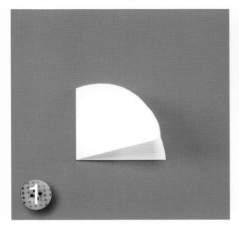

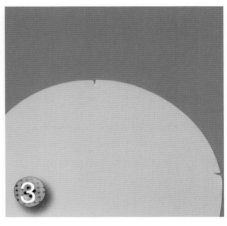

Place the round item on a piece of paper and trace around it. Cut the circle out and fold it into quarters. Mark the quarter points.

Unfold the circle pattern, place it on template plastic and draw around it. Mark the quarter points.

Cut the template out and make small V-shaped cuts at the quarter marks.

Using a Compass

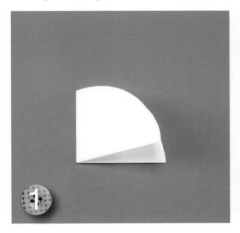

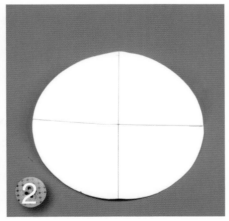

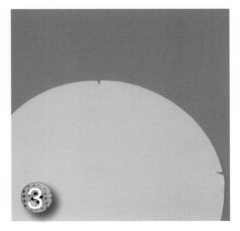

Set the compass for the size circle you need. Draw the circle on paper and cut out. Fold the circle in quarters.

Unfold and mark the crease lines with a pencil.

Place the circular paper pattern onto template plastic and draw around it. Mark the quarter points. Cut the template out and make small V-shaped cuts at the quarter marks.
Note: You may wish to transfer the crease lines from the paper circle to the template.

Marking the Teacup Design

Circles

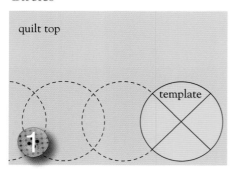

Mark the overlapping circles in rows working from the center out toward the edge of the quilt top. In row one, align the lines on each circle with the one drawn previously.

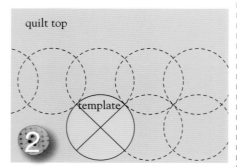

In row two, overlap the second row of circles with the first row, as shown.

Wavy Lines

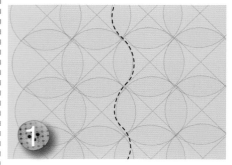

Mark the outer edges of the circle template to create a wavy line along the length of the quilt top. Repeat along the entire length of the quilt top.

Note: You do not need to stitch the teacup design in circles. Quilt in a continuous wavy line and when complete they will form interlocking circles.
You may also quilt a selection of wavy lines to create other designs.

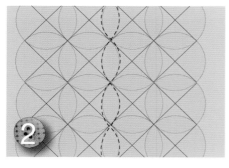

Move the circle template and draw on the outer edge again to make a pumpkin seed design. Repeat along the entire length of the quilt top.

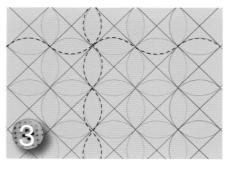

Repeat step 1 to mark the width of the quilt top.

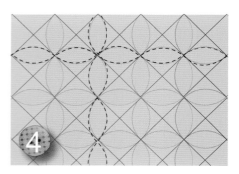

Repeat step 2 to finish marking the width of the quilt top.

Clam Shell

The intricate Clam Shell design is simply one half circle on top of another. Use a semi-circle to mark the design in rows starting at an outside edge of the quilt. If you use a large template, you can double the lines for more emphasis.

To make the circle template refer to Making a Circle Template on page 37.

Marking the Clam Shell Design

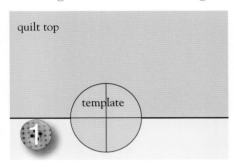

Align the circle template with a straight line on the quilt top. Use an outside edge of the quilt or the seamlines of the quilt rows. Our example uses the bottom edge of the quilt top.

Draw a row of semi-circles along the bottom edge of the quilt. The designs should be butted up next to each other.

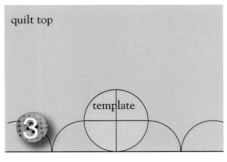

To mark the second row, align the center lines on the template with the top of the drawn semi-circles.

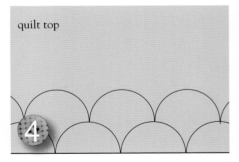

Continue to mark rows of semi-circles in this manner.
When you quilt the pattern, stitch the lines in the same order they were marked.

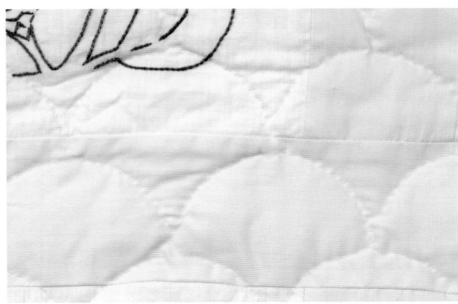

A clam shell design was used in this quilt without regard to block or sashing placement. Its all over use unifies the look of the quilt top.

Cables

Cable designs fulfill many of the same requirements as utility quilting. They can be quilted in one direction and marked on a quilt as an all over design, as well as being used in borders. Cables are simple to make and can easily be created from an ellipse-shaped template cut from paper.

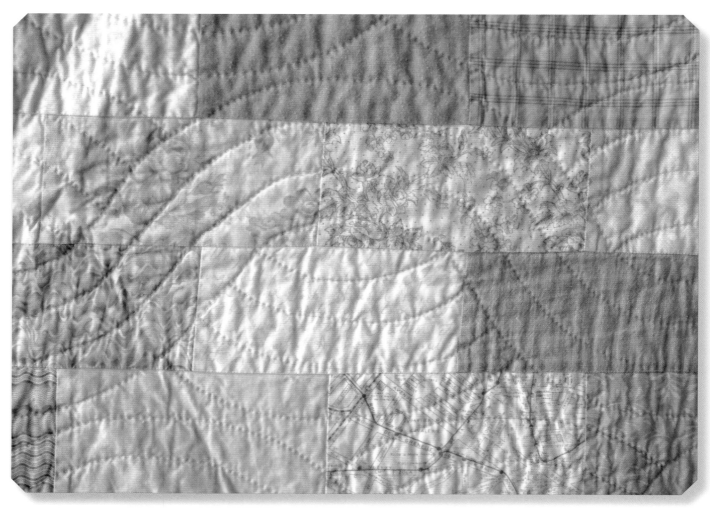

Bricks quilt, 2008
Pieced and hand quilted by Carolyn Forster

This variation of the cable design unifies the rectangular block. It adds softness to an otherwise rigid design.

Making a Cable Template

The template for any cable design is a simple ellipse shape with the middle cut out. They are easy to make with paper and scissors. Don't worry if it is not perfect the first time, just get more paper and try again.

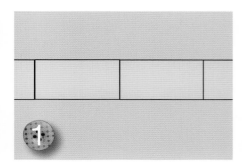

Cut a strip of paper the width of the cable desired and the length of the quilt. This will help you get the proportions right.

Fold the paper in half lengthwise. Then fold it in quarters and keep folding until you have a rectangle. If the rectangle is too short, refold the paper into thirds. This will give you different proportions and a longer rectangle.

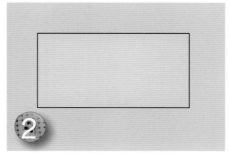

Cut one of the rectangles from the paper.

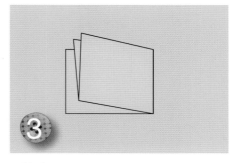

Fold the rectangle into quarters.

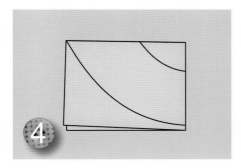

Mark or cut the shape as shown.

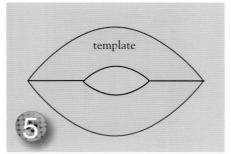

template

Unfold the ellipse and draw around the shape on scrap paper to see how the cable forms.
If you need to make adjustments, trim the ellipse or cut a new one. When you are happy with the shape, trace it onto template plastic.

Tip
Tape together newspaper to make a big piece of paper quickly.

Marking the Cable Design

More than one quilting design can be drawn from the simple ellipse shape. To mark the whole quilt, ignore the piecing as you are marking unless you are using the seams as a guide. See the examples shown for design marking ideas.

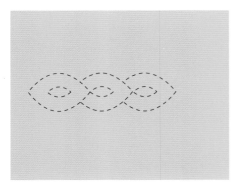

Overlap the ellipse templates.

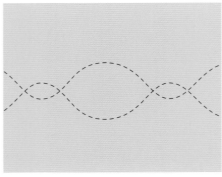

Mark the outline and inner shape.

Mark only the outline of the ellipse.

Overlap the template and freehand draw a line in the center.

Overlap and omit some of the lines to create a rope effect.

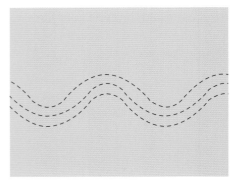

Omit some lines to create a Ric Rac design.

Straight Line Design

A Straight Line design is the simplest way to quilt a quilt and can be worked over the entire top. With some imagination you can reinvent the straight line on every quilt so no two look the same.

Marking the Straight Line Design

You do not need a template to mark the straight line design on your quilt top. Use your acrylic quilting ruler and a hera marker to mark the lines when there is not a natural line to follow from the piecing.

Dividing Up the Quilt Top

Instead of drawing lines over the complete top, divide the top into quarters. Fill each quarter section with lines going in different directions. Use the following examples to get you started.

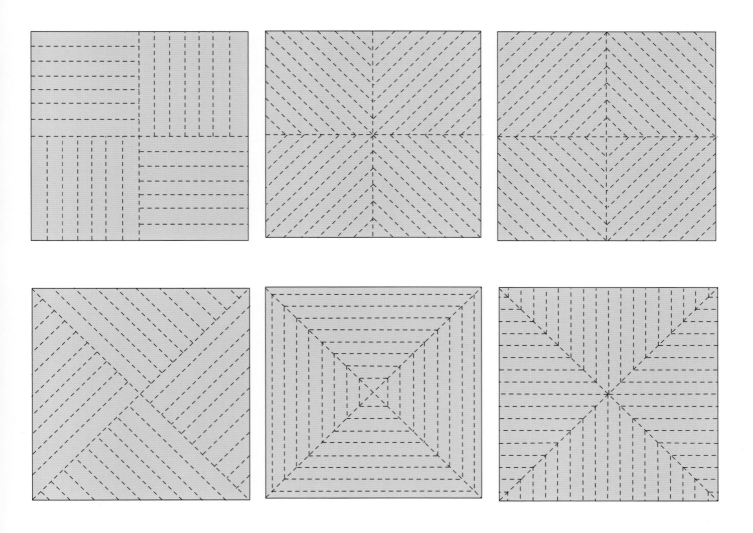

Straight Line Design Variations

Any straight line design can be quilted with single, double or even triple lines. This is a simple way to give the quilting design more emphasis.

Straight lines

The quilting on this 1930's quilt follows the lines of the pieced blocks.

The quilting in the border of the 19th century scrap quilt above was done with double lines drawn at a 45-degree angle for more emphasis.

Mark single, horizontal straight lines on the quilt top.

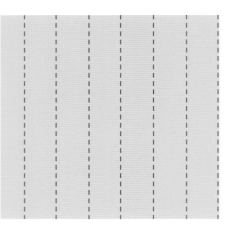

Mark single, vertical straight lines on the quilt top.

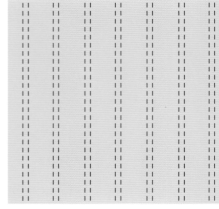

Mark double, vertical straight lines on the quilt top.

Squares

Single, straight lines create squares across the top of this antique quilt.

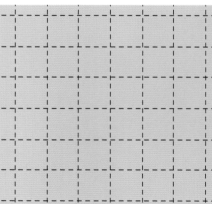

Use straight lines at 90-degrees to mark single squares across the quilt top.

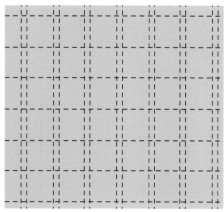

Combine single and double lines for a more interesting quilting design.

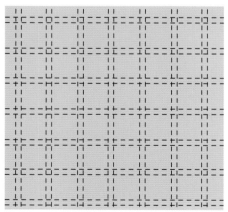

Mark sets of straight lines to create double-line squares.

Diamonds or Cross Hatch Designs

Straight lines are used to create a variety of Diamond and Cross Hatch quilting designs.

Mark single diagonal lines at a 45-degree angle across the quilt.

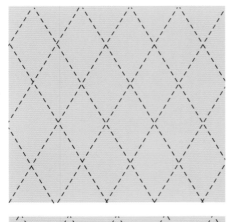

Mark single diagonal lines at 60-degrees for longer diamonds.

Mark a straight horizontal line across the 60-degree diamond grid to create equilateral triangles.

Diamond Variations

Combine different sets of lines to create various types of diamonds.

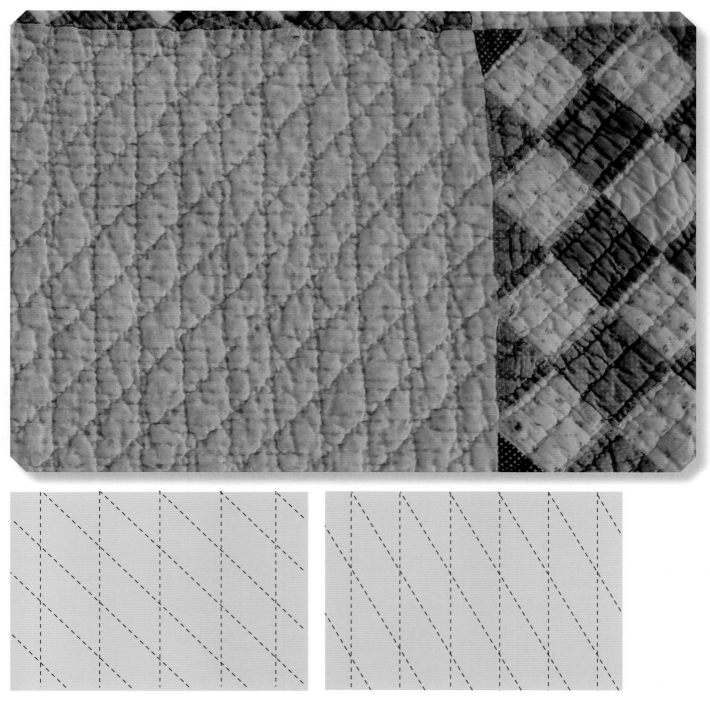

Mark one set of lines at 90-degrees and another set at 45-degrees to create the diamond pattern variation above.

Mark 90-degree and 60-degree lines for longer diamonds..

Freehand Quilting Designs – No Marking

Freehand quilting designs, or designs that follow the general lines and shapes in the patchwork, do not need to be marked.

Quilting in the ditch

Stitch in the seam line of the pieced patchwork. Big Stitch quilting works well in the ditch and doesn't get lost on the quilt top. This quilt was stitched in the ditch along the seam lines of the outer border pieces.

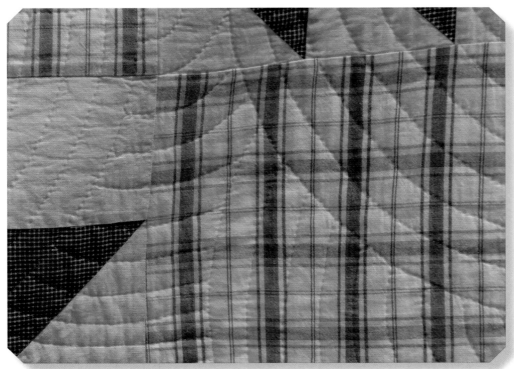

Elbow quilting

Mark the first small arc freehand or use your thumb as a guide. All the increasing larger arcs are sewn by eye and gauged by the length of the needle or the width of your thumb.

Outline quilting

Quilt ¼" from the seams of the patchwork. This way you will not have
to bring the needle through more layers of fabric than necessary.

Borders

Even though we are talking about quilting a quilt with an all over design, when the quilt has a border we can use a different design in it to add more interest. The marking and quilting is still quick if you use the designs you have already learned.

The sampler quilt, shown, is cross hatched over the quilt center. In contrast, the outer border has a simple cable design.

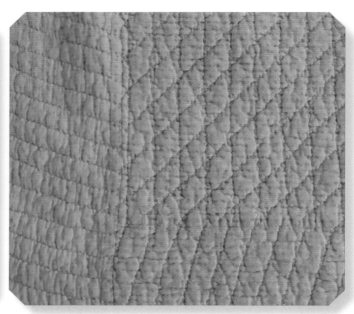

The antique quilt, above, has a version of Hanging Diamonds over the quilt center and single slanted lines in the border.

This scrappy quilt from the 1880's is cross hatched through the center. Double lines are quilted at a 45-degree angle in the border.

This quilt was quilted in the border with single 45-degree lines.

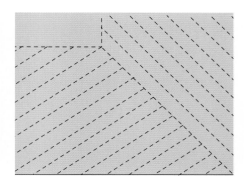

Mark border with single 45-degree lines.

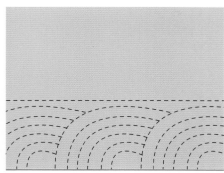

Wave and clam shell designs give a sense of movement in a border.

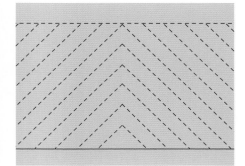

Mark lines that meet in the center of the border.

Corners

Quilters of the past didn't worry about their designs wrapping around the border's corner. A few examples are provided to give you some corner quilting ideas.

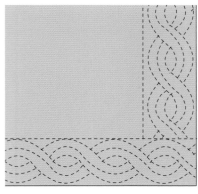

The cable design on this border trails off the edge.

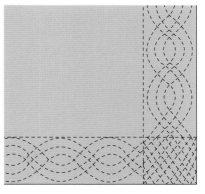

This cable design stops and cross hatching fills the corner square.

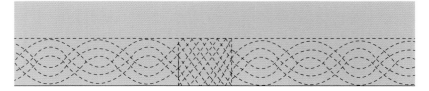

If quilters had a design that traveled around the corner, but would not meet in the middle of the border, they would ignore this by blocking out a square in the center of the border and filling it with another design.

The Stitches

Utility quilting uses bigger and bolder stitches than fine hand quilting. Although many quilters prefer finishing their quilts with stitches, you can speed the process along by tying your quilt with thick threads and a variety of knots.

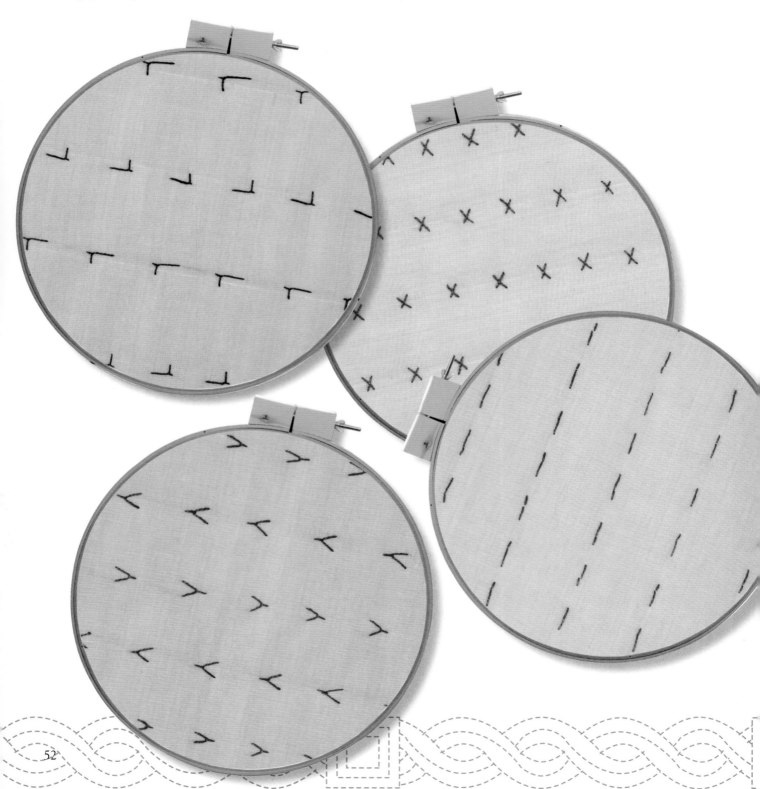

Preparing to Stitch

I use the same starting and ending method for my utility quilting and fine hand quilting stitches. I have found this method works well no matter which stitch I am using. Refer to page 14 for information on my favorite and most often used stitching supplies.

Threading the Needle

Before you begin stitching you must learn how to thread your needle and securely start and end your stitch. If this is done correctly, you will not be wasting time going back over stitches that have come undone.

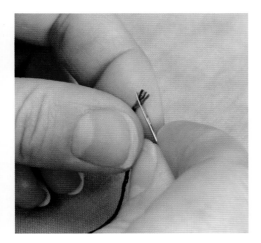

Cut your thread the length of your arm. This may not seem very long, but it will make the stitching process easier. The thread is less likely to become tangled and knotted. It also allows a more ergonomic stretch of the arm when stitching. Instead pulling a long thread upward, you will be pivoting from the elbow, which is less tiring.

When threading the needle I always find it easier to hold the thread and put the needle over the thread, rather than trying to poke a piece of thread through a needle's eye.

Tip

If you find threading the needle difficult, invest in a needle threader. If you are having trouble pulling the needle through the layers when using bulkier threads, try a Needle Grabber™ to grip the needle and pull it through the layers. Refer to Stitching Supplies on page 14.

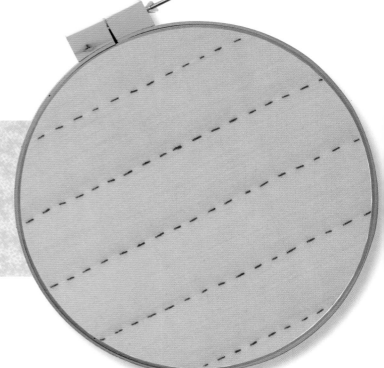

Starting the Stitch

Cut a length of thread as long as your arm. Tie a knot in the end you just cut. Thread the unknotted end through the needle eye.

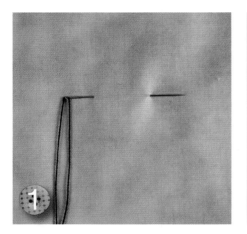

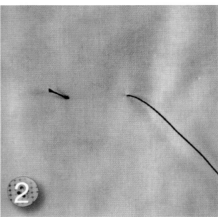

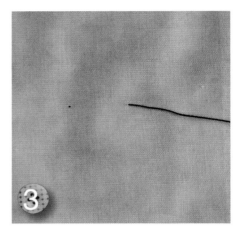

Determine where you want to begin quilting. Insert the needle through the top layer of fabric and batting a small distance from where you will begin quilting. Bring the needle point up at the spot you want to begin your stitches.

The knot should now be laying on the top layer of fabric.

To embed the knot in the batting, gently pull the thread until the knot 'pops' down into the batting.
The embedded thread will be quilted over with your chosen stitch. This adds an extra layer of security for the thread.

Tip
If the knot is stubborn and won't pull through the fabric, use the point of the needle and poke the weave of the fabric to expand the hole where the knot needs to go through. Gently pull the thread until the knot goes into the batting. Use the needle to push the threads back in place.

Ending the stitch

When you are finished stitching or the thread is running out, you will need to secure your ending stitches. Leave approximately 5" – 6" of thread to end your stitch.

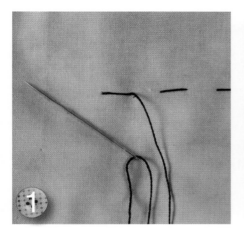

To secure the last stitch, go all the way through to the back of the quilt with the needle. Bring the needle up at the beginning of the stitch.

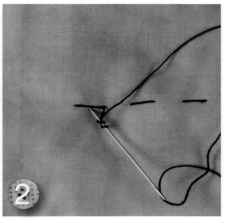

Pull the thread through and wrap it around the needle three times, keeping the thread close to the quilt.

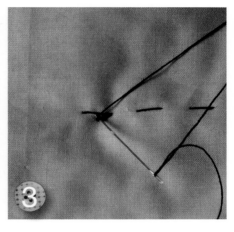

Push the needle into the middle of the last stitch, just underneath it and through the top layer and batting.

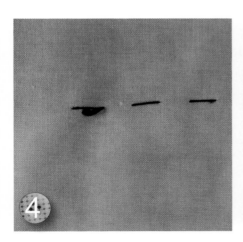

Travel approximately a needle's length away from the stitching, and bring the needle back up to the surface. As you pull the thread a knot will form.

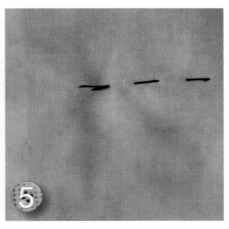

Gently pull the knot through to embed it in the batting. Snip the thread close to the quilt top.

Big Stitch Quilting

Big stitch quilting is a bolder style of quilting. The designs are usually more widely spaced, therefore needing fewer lines and less time to quilt. It also uses a thicker thread and longer stitches. The stitch length is often longer on the top layer of the quilt and smaller on the bottom layer. This style of stitching gives the quilt a chunkier, primitive, more masculine feel. It is sometimes referred to as Depression Stitching or Naïve Quilting.

Heavier Fabrics, Bigger Stitches

Many of the quilts we see from our ancestors or in museums were pieced from heavy wool fabrics. Therefore, the bigger stitches and thicker threads were needed, since fine thread and small stitches would not have held the layers together.

In some depression era (1930s) quilts the thick quilting thread was believed to be the sewing thread used to hold flour sacks together before they were cut and sewn into quilts. Using the bigger quilting stitch was another way to get the job done faster, when flour sack quilts was one of the only affordable ways to keep warm at night.

A variety of stitches are shown on the following pages. Choose the ones that will enhance your quilt top and consider these tips while stitching.

Big Stitch Tips

- There are no rules when it comes to the number of utility stitches per inch, but as a general guideline try four to five stitches per inch. If you are using thicker threads the stitches can be bigger.

- As you stitch, try to keep a rhythm of creating large, even stitches that go through all three layers.

- Some people keep the needle hand still and move the finger on the underside of the quilt to create the stitches. Others do the exact opposite. Try different motions to find what is comfortable and creates the even stitches you want.

- I find it helpful to have a thimble on the middle finger of my needle hand for pushing the needle through and a ridged thimble on the index finger of my hand under the quilt.

- The finger under the quilt pushes the layers up creating a little hill with the ridge of the thimble. The needle is pushed against it to make the stitch.

- When there is approximately 6" of thread left in the needle, end your stitch and start a new length of thread.

- If you will be using a hoop when quilting, keep in mind that you do not want the hoop too tight. It should keep the layers flat but allow enough flexibility so you can move the needle up and down.

Methodist Knot

The Methodist Knot stitch adds texture as it holds the three layers of the quilt together. The stitches work up quickly and you can develop a nice stitching rhythm.

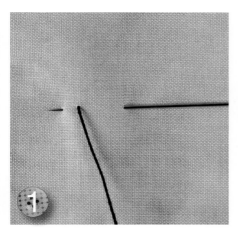

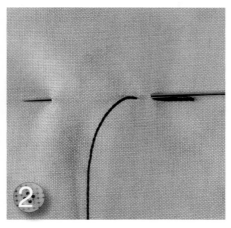

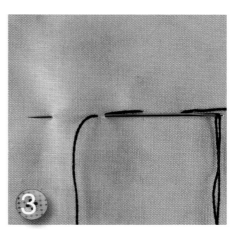

Review Starting the Stitch on page 54 to thread the needle and embed the knot in the batting along the line you will be stitching over. Come up through the top layer and insert the needle down through all three layers. Bring the needle back up about one third length of the back stitch in front of it.

Push the needle down into the batting, creating a small back stitch. Travel the needle along to the next stitch.

Continue stitching in this way. End the stitch on the small backstitch, referring to Ending the Stitch on page 55.

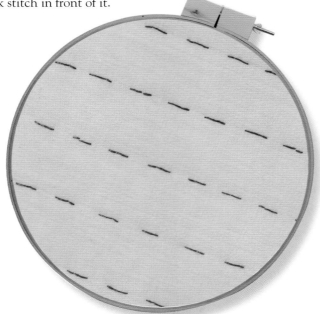

Modified Backstitch

The Modified Backstitch is worked in the same way as the Methodist Knot stitch. However, the Modified Backstitch gives you a slightly bolder look.

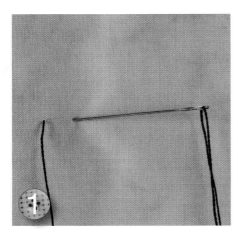

Review Starting the Stitch on page 54 to thread the needle and embed the knot in the batting along the line you will be stitching over. Make the first stitch going down through all three layers of the quilt.

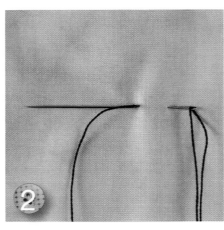

Bring the needle back up where the stitch started.

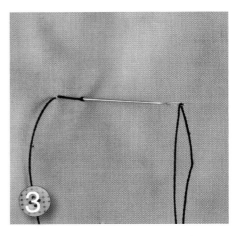

Push the needle back down into the batting where the first stitch finished.

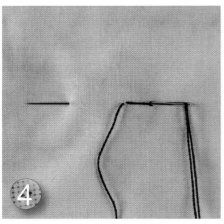

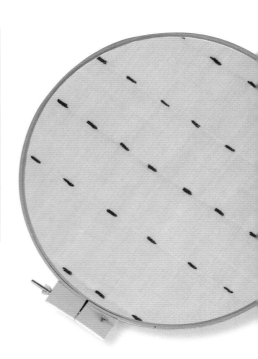

Travel the needle through the batting. Bring it up the desired distance away to begin the next stitch.

When there is approximately 6" of thread left in the needle, end your stitch and start a new length of thread. Refer to Ending the Stitch on page 55.

Crows Footing

The Crows Footing stitch is similar to the embroidery fly stitch. It is most comfortably worked toward the quilter.

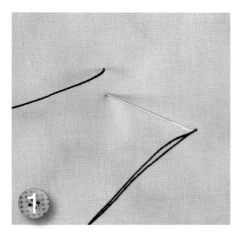
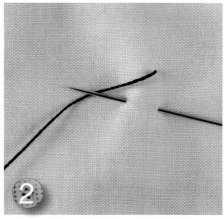
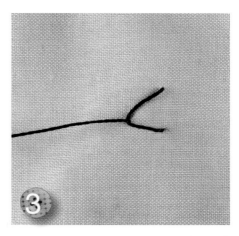

Review Starting the Stitch on page 54 to thread the needle and embed the knot in the batting along the line you will be stitching over. Working the stitches toward you, insert the needle down into all three layers of the quilt approximately ½" from the start of the stitch.

Bring the needle back up approximately ½" below in the middle of the gap.

As you bring the needle up and pull the thread there will be a loop. Bring the needle up inside the loop and tighten the thread.

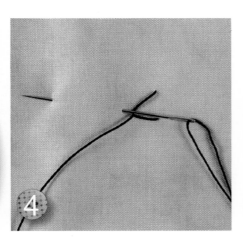
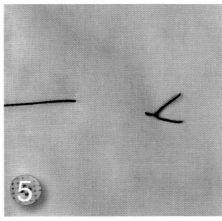
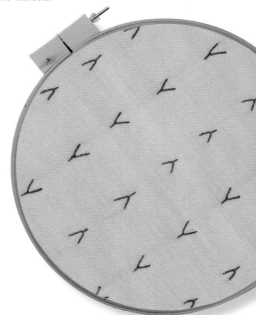

Insert the needle into the top and batting, approximately ½" from the end of the stitch. Travel a needle's length from the first stitch and begin the next stitch. When there is approximately 6" of thread left in the needle, end your stitch and start a new length of thread. Refer to Ending the Stitch on page 55.

Buttonhole Stitch

The Buttonhole stitch is a slight variation of the Crows Footing stitch. It is also easiest to achieve by stitching toward you..

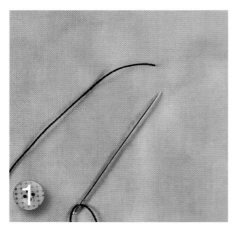

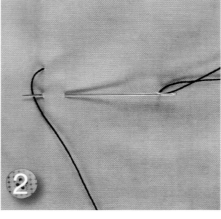

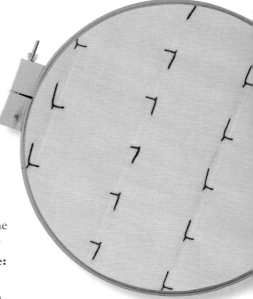

Review Starting the Stitch on page 54 to thread the needle and embed the knot in the batting along the line you will be stitching over.

Working the stitches toward you, insert the needle down into all three layers of the quilt approximately ½" below and slightly to the right of the start of the stitch. **Note:** If you are left-handed, your stitch will be slightly to the left of the start of the stitch.

Bring the needle back up, below where the thread first came out of the quilt. As you pull the thread there will be a loop. Make sure the needle is inside the loop. Tighten the thread.

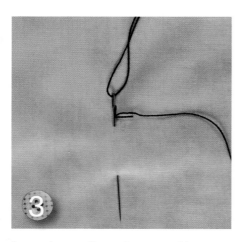

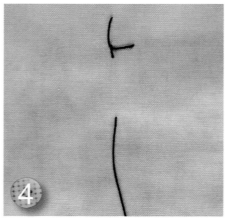

Insert the needle in the top and batting and make a small stitch to keep the loop in place.

Travel the needle through the batting the desired distance to begin the next stitch. When there is approximately 6" of thread left in the needle, end your stitch and start a new length of thread. Refer to Ending the Stitch on page 55.

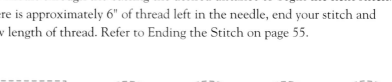

Running Cross Stitch

The Running Cross stitch is similar to the Japanese Sashiko stitch called Ten (juujizashi). In this stitch rows of running stitches intersect to make little crosses. The stitches here are worked one at a time.

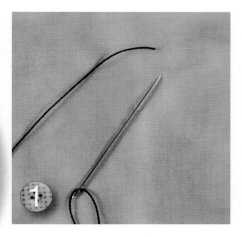 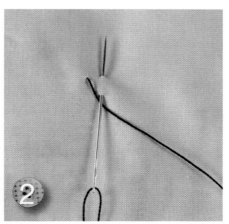 

Review Starting the Stitch on page 54 to thread the needle and embed the knot in the batting along the line you will be stitching over.

Insert the needle through all three layers of the quilt forming a diagonal stitch. Bring the needle back up at the top and to the right of the beginning stitch.

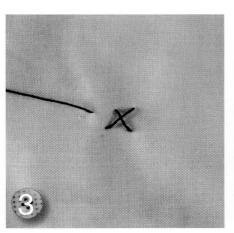 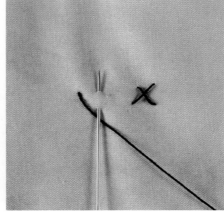

Insert the needle down into the top and batting, forming an 'x' with the thread. Travel the needle to the start of the next stitch.

When there is approximately 6" of thread left in the needle, end your stitch and start a new length of thread. Refer to Ending the Stitch on page 55.

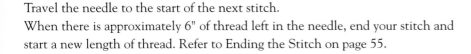

Knots and Tying

One of the simplest ways to secure the layers of a quilt is to tie them. This can be done with a single or double thread and a simple reef knot, or more elaborately with multiple threads and more complicated knots. Experiment with different threads, thicknesses, and tail lengths to see which work best with your project.

Creating a Grid

Generally you will tie your quilt at the seams of the blocks. This provides an easy grid to follow. If you do not have a pattern to follow, you can create a grid.

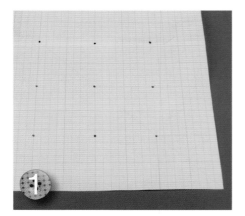

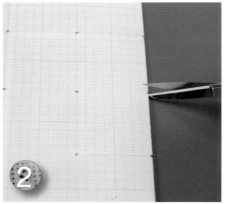

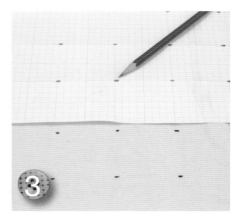

Using a piece of 18" x 18" quilter's graph paper, mark an even grid using the lines on the paper and a pencil.

When you are happy with your grid, fold the paper along a row of marks, and snip a hole for each mark. Continue until all the pencil marks are replaced by a hole.

Place the graph paper over the quilt. Use a pencil and the holes and mark where you want to tie the quilt.

Tip
If you do not have a large enough piece of quilter's graph paper, tape sheets together to create the size you need. You may also use a piece of checked gingham cloth. This will give you a larger sheet of grid to work with.

This vintage scrap quilt has a soft, thick batting. The layers have been tied at regular intervals with thick cotton thread.

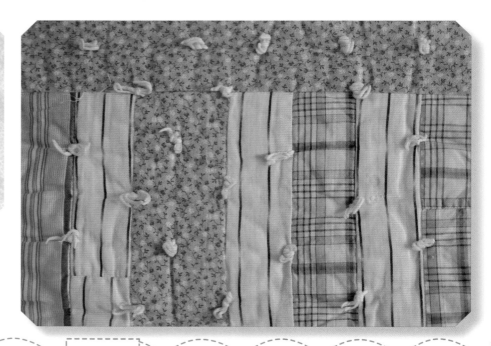

Reef Knot/ Square Knot

I most commonly use a double thread and a reef/square knot when I tie my quilts. When using this method you can start with a long thread in the needle, often twice the length of your arm.

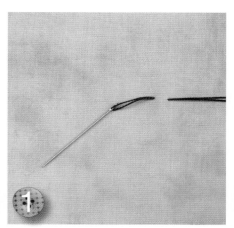

Thread your needle with a double piece of thread approximately twice the length of your arm. Insert the needle through all three layers of the quilt, coming come up 1/4" away from the start.

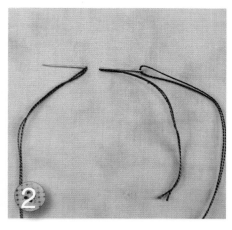

Re-insert the needle in the same place, through all the layers.

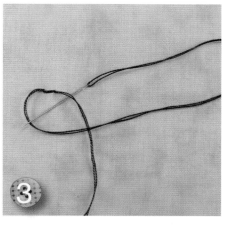

Bring the needle up. Loop the left thread over the right and through the loop.

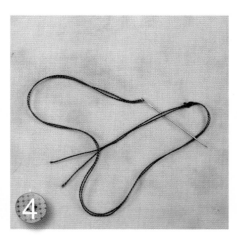

Pull tight and repeat, passing the right thread over the left and through the loop.

Pull tight and cut off the excess thread.

Surgeon's Knot

The Surgeon's Knot is similar to the Reef Knot, but instead of the thread going through the loop once, it goes through twice each time. This results in more twists and a longer, flatter knot.

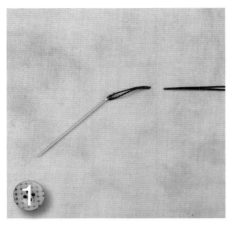

Thread your needle with a double piece of thread approximately twice the length of your arm. Insert the needle through all three layers of the quilt, coming come up 1/4" away from the start.

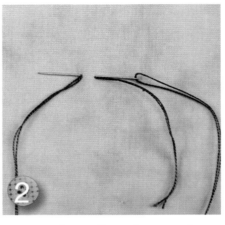

Re-insert the needle in the same place, through all the layers.

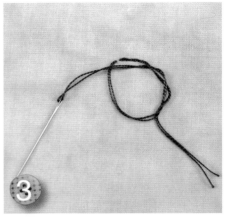

Bring the needle up. Pass the thread through the loop twice.

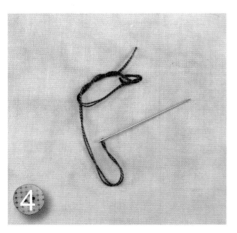

Pull tight and pass the thread through the loop twice the other way.

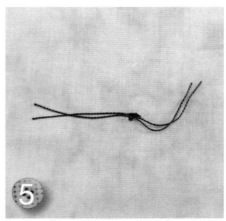

Pull tight and cut off the excess thread.

Continuous Ties

Use Continuous Ties when you do not want to tie and snip every knot.

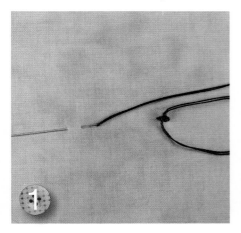

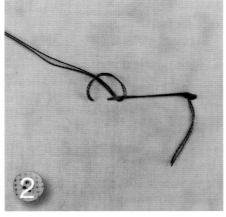

Make a Reef Knot referring to the instructions on page 63. After completing the knot, insert the needle through all three layers at the next point for the knot, coming up to the top of the quilt.

Take the needle through the loop from front to back and then back under the original 'line' of thread.

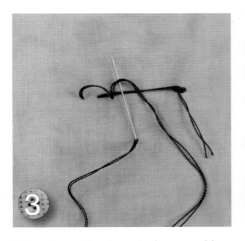

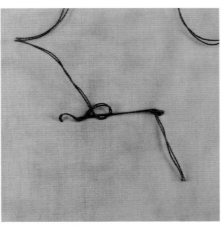

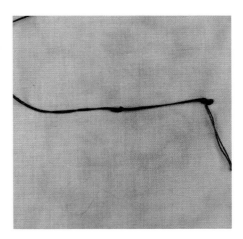

Take the needle through the second loop and pull firmly to tighten the knot. Continue on to the next stitch. When the thread runs out, or you have enough knots, go back and snip the joining threads.

Decatur Knot

The Decatur Knot can be considered a stitch since it is a sewn knot. The starting knot is embedded in the batting. It has no loose ends and is sewn continuously. You end the knot as you would for Big Stitch style quilting. The Decatur Knot works well over joined seams. This knot can be stitched two ways. Use the one that works best for you.

Method 1

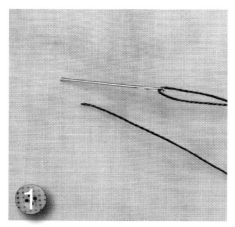

Bring the needle up through the top of the quilt and then insert it down through all three layers to make a diagonal stitch.

Bring the needle up through all the layers to the right of the diagonal stitch.

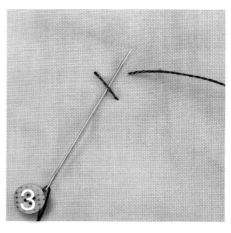

Insert the needle under the stitch moving the needle away from you.

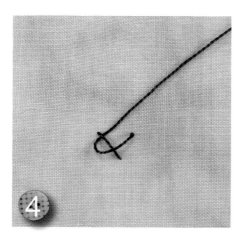

Pull the thread through firmly to form a 'twist'.

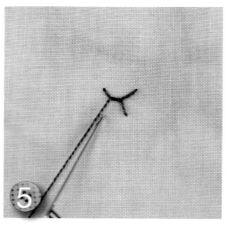

Insert the needle through the batting to complete the Decatur Knot.

Decatur Knot

This method creates a slight knot or bump in the stitch, rather than a twist as in Method 1.

Method 2

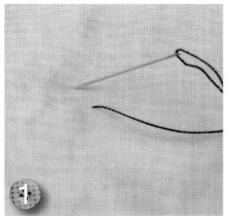

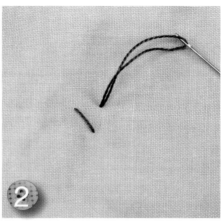

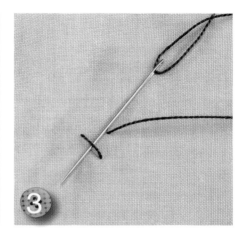

Bring the needle up through the top of the quilt and then insert it down through all three layers pulling the thread tight to make a diagonal stitch. Bring the needle back up through all the layers to the right of the stitch just made.

Insert the needle under the diagonal stitch.

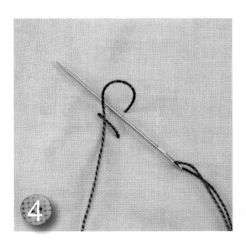

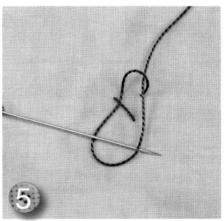

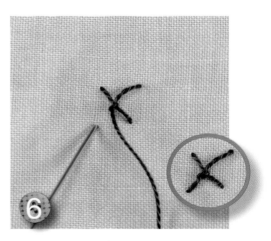

Bring the needle up and through the loop formed at the top right corner of the diagonal stitch. Pull the needle through leaving a medium-size loop.

Insert the needle through the loop and pull tight to form a knot on the diagonal stitch. It is helpful to hold the top right corner of the stitch while tightening.

Insert the needle into the batting at the lower left corner to complete the Decatur Knot.

Bow Knot

A Bow Knot has loops as well as loose ends. To ensure the bow does not come undone, the loops are tied together.

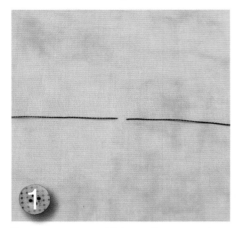

Begin as you would for making a reef knot. Be sure you leave enough loose thread to tie the bow.

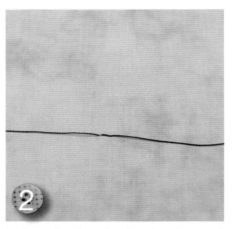

Tighten the thread and make a bow in the usual way. Pull tight.

Take the loops and tie together as in the first part of the reef knot. Pull firmly.

Hidden Ties

You can hide the ties by threading the loose threads into the needle and inserting into the batting of the quilt. Draw the needle out, approximately 1" from the tie. Cut the surplus threads.

You can also hide the threads on the back of the quilt. This is just the reverse of regular tying and leaves the loose threads of the knot on the back rather than the front of the quilt.

Buttons

Buttons can be added for decorative effect when tying a quilt. See the examples below. The buttons will also help stop the thread from wearing through the quilt layers and ripping. You can use any buttons that will withstand laundering.
Note: Always keep in mind that buttons should not be used on quilts for young children as they can choke on buttons if they come loose.

Felt

Felt disks can be used as an alternative to buttons. They can be cut from purchased felt, your own handmade felt, or pre-cut shapes. The shapes, usually squares or circles, can be cut with a crimped or plain edge depending on the effect required. Experiment with two felt disks layered on top of each other, or a layered felt disk and a button.

Machine Stitching and Decorative Stitches

Sewing machines can do more than just sew straight lines. If your machine has decorative stitches, use them to 'tie' the quilt layers together.

You can also use three or four zig-zag stitches to hold the quilt layers together. Tie off the loose ends on the back of the quilt and sew the threads into the batting, or secure by stitching over the area.

Binding and Other Edge Finish Techniques

Be open to trying different binding techniques on your quilts. Determine the amount of time you wish to spend on the binding process and this will help you decide which technique to use.

This antique quilt is an example of the Back Over to Front binding technique.

The Stretched Hexagon quilt on page 110 features a Turned Through Edge Finish.

The maker of this 19th century quilt used the Turned Over to Front binding method.

Refer to Getting Started, Binding Supplies on page 13 before beginning.

Cutting the Binding on the Straight-of-Grain

The bindings shown are cut on the fabric's straight-of-grain.

Advantages to this are:

- It is easier and quicker.
- You can use pre-cut 2½" strips.
- Helps straighten the edges of the quilt.
- More economical use of fabric.
- Folding for a double binding adds durability and strength.

Machine Stitched Continuous Binding

The Machine Stitched Continuous binding technique has virtually no hand finishing so you can quickly turn your binding with your machine.

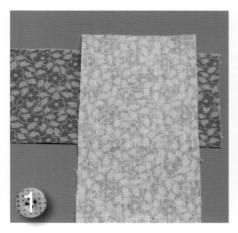

Cut strips of fabric for the binding 2½" wide. Lay one of the strips right side up on a flat surface. Place a second strip wrong side up on the first, as shown.

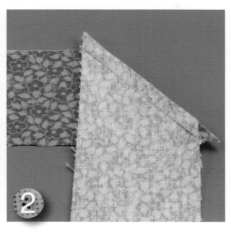

Draw a diagonal line from corner to corner beginning at the right corner where the strips meet. Sew on the marked line and trim ¼" from the sewn line.

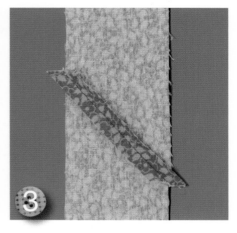

Press the seams open. Continue to sew strips together in this way to make one continuous binding strip.

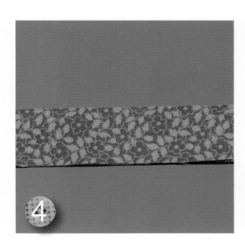

Press the length of the continuous binding strip in half, wrong sides together.

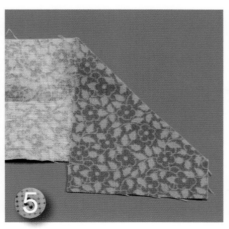

Unfold the binding strip and fold one end at a 45-degree angle. Press.

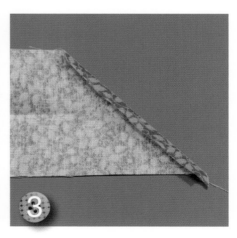

Trim ¼" from the pressed fold.

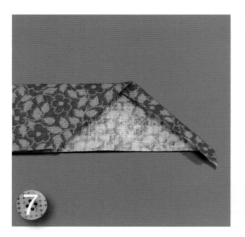

Refold and press the binding strip.

Trim the backing and batting even with the quilt top. Make sure all the layers are square and even.

The binding will be attached to the back of the quilt first. Align the raw angled edge of the binding strip with the raw edge of the quilt back at the center of one of the sides. Begin to sew the binding to the quilt about ½" away from the angled edge.

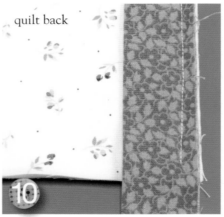

Using the walking foot sew toward the first corner, stopping ¼" away. Secure with a few backstitches and remove the quilt top from under the presser foot.

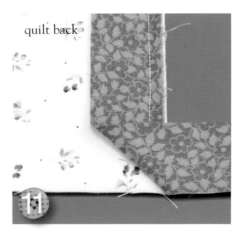

Fold the binding strip to form a 45-degree mitered corner.

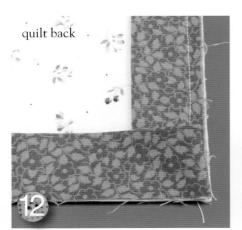

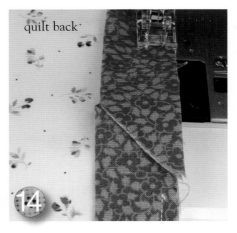

12 Bring the binding strip over to align with the raw edge of the quilt top.

13 Begin sewing from the edge of the quilt and binding to secure the fold. Continue sewing, repeating the process at each corner.

14 Stop sewing when you are approximately 6" away from the beginning angled end of the binding strip. Trim the binding as needed to tuck into the angled end.

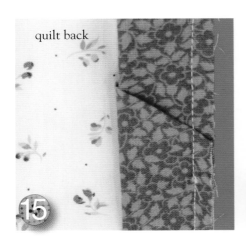

15 Continue sewing to the beginning stitches. Backstitch to secure.

The stitching on the back of the quilt will be similar to the example shown.

16 Turn the quilt over and fold the binding to the front, covering the raw edges and overlapping the machine stitching on the front of the quilt. Pin in place, mitering the binding at the corners.

17 Stitch around the edge of the binding a scant $1/8$" away from the fold. At each corner, stitch up to the miter, lift the machine foot, leaving the needle in the work and turn the quilt to sew along the next side. Continue until all sides are sewn down.

Square Corner Binding

The Square Corner binding technique allows you to use pre-cut fabric strips, such as Jelly Rolls®. Each side of the quilt is bound separately with a different fabric, providing extra strength to the edges of your quilt. This is also a great way to use your scraps and create an interesting binding. Square Corner binding is sewn on the machine and finished by hand.

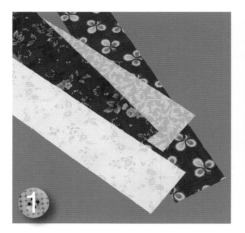

Cut strips of binding 2½" wide and join them diagonally following steps 1 - 3 in Machine Stitching Continuous binding on page 71.

In this example I used four different fabrics. Remember this is a great way to use your scraps or precut fabrics.

You will need four continuous strips approximately 2" longer than each side of the quilt. Press the length of the continuous binding strip in half, wrong sides together.

Match the raw edges of the binding strip and one side of the quilt. Begin sewing the strip to the side of the quilt using a ¼" seam allowance.

When you reach the end, trim the binding even with the bottom edge of the quilt top.

Repeat this process on the opposite side of the quilt.

Trim the extra backing and batting even with the raw edge of the binding.

Finger press the binding away from the quilt top.

On an unfinished edge of the quilt top, align the raw edge of a remaining binding strip even with the top of the attached binding strip.

Tip

Use your ruler when trimming if your seam allowance was on the generous side.

Square Corner Binding continued

Sew with a ¼" seam allowance to the end of the adjacent attached binding strip. Trim the excess binding even with the attached binding strip. Repeat on the remaining side of the quilt top.

Trim the extra batting even with the raw edge of the binding. Repeat on the remaining side of the quilt top.

quilt back

Turn the quilt top so the back is facing up.

quilt back

At the corners trim away the extra fabric and batting to make turning the binding easier.

Fold one binding strip over to the back side of the quilt and pin in place.

Fold the adjacent binding strip over to the back of the quilt and pin. Fold the corners so the raw edges are concealed. Repeat on all sides of the quilt top.

Slip stitch the binding in place along the folded edge. Be sure to sew along the open edges at the corners.

Back Over to Front Binding

The Back Over to Front binding technique is the perfect way to use extra backing fabric. It also gives the edges a tidy look that can be sewn by hand or machine. Choose a backing fabric that complements the front of the quilt for a coordinated look. For an old-fashioned feel use muslin or calico on the quilt back.

When the quilt layers have been quilted, trim the batting to the same size as the quilt top.

Trim the backing fabric leaving 1" around all edges of the quilt top.

Fold the backing fabric in half, wrong sides together, so the raw edge aligns with the batting and quilt top.

Tip
Experiment with different widths of binding to see what suits your quilt. Wider bindings can accommodate a row of big stitch quilting or running cross stitch.

4 Turn the folded edge over so it is laying on the quilt top. Pin in place. If you prefer you may use hemming clips instead of pins.

Square corner finish

Miter corner finish

5 At the corners you can create a square corner or miter corner finish.

Square Corner Finish

6 For square corners continue to fold the adjacent edge tucking in the raw edge of the backing fabric. Pin in place.

Miter Corner Finish

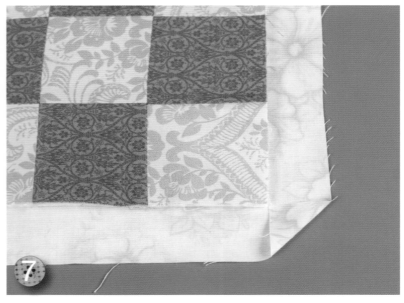

7 For a mitered corner, the long edges of the backing fabric should not be folded yet. Fold the corner of the backing fabric in half, wrong sides together, toward the corner of the quilt top and batting.

Turn the folded edge over so it is laying on the quilt top. Pin in place.

Fold the long edge of the backing fabric in half, wrong sides together. Align the raw edge with the batting and quilt top.

Turn the folded edge over so it is laying on the quilt top. Pin in place.

Repeat on the adjacent side to complete the miter.

Sew the binding in place using a slip stitch for an invisible finish. You may also choose to use a big stitch or a machine stitch.

Turned Through Edge Finish

The Turned Through Edge Finish binding technique actually lets you bind your quilt before it is quilted! It works well with quilts that do not require batting, such as those backed with Polar Fleece or Minky™. It also works well for quilts that are going to be tied or big stitch quilted.

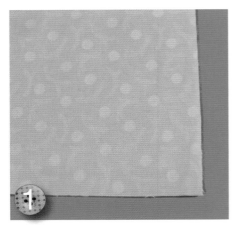

Smooth the batting out on a flat surface and secure with tape if needed. Place the quilt backing, right side up, on top of the batting. Smooth out any wrinkles.

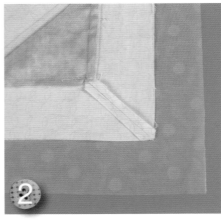

Center the quilt top, wrong side down, on the backing fabric.

Pin the three layers together around the edge of the quilt top. Place the pins perpendicular to the edge. Leave a 6" gap in the middle of one side in order to turn the quilt right side out after sewing.

Note: If you are making a two layer quilt without batting, smooth and secure the backing fabric, right side up, to a flat surface. Center the quilt top, wrong side up, on top of the backing fabric.

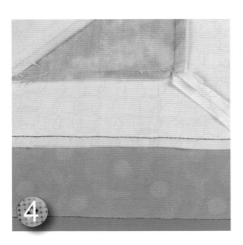

With a walking foot, begin stitching around the edge of the quilt top using a ¼" seam allowance. Backstitch the beginning few stitches to secure them. Remove the pins as you come to them.

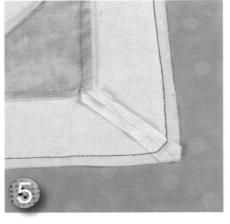

As you come to each corner, stitch two or three stitches across it for a neater corner when you turn the quilt through. Backstitch your ending stitches to secure them.

Note: We used contrasting thread for demonstration purposes. Use a matching thread in your project.

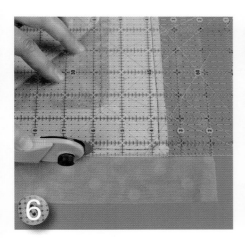

Trim the batting and quilt back to leave a ¼" seam allowance.

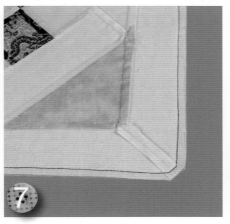

Snip diagonally across the corners through all three layers.

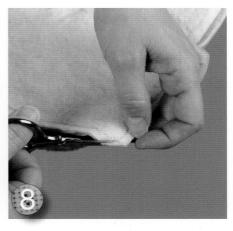

Using a pair of small sharp scissors trim the batting close to the sewing line around the entire quilt top.

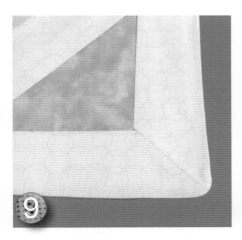

Turn the quilt right side out, poking the corners out and 'rolling' the seam between your thumb and forefinger to help it lay flat. You may use pins or hemming clips to keep the edges flat. Sew the quilt opening closed using a slip stitch.

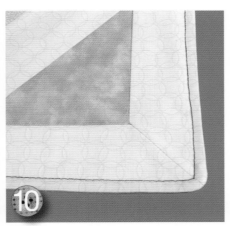

To keep the edge in place permanently, use your sewing machine and walking foot. Increase the length of the stitch used for piecing and sew along the edge of the quilt where the bulk of the seam allowance ends.

For hand stitching, use Big Stitch Quilting (page 56) and sew along the outside edge of the quilt just along where the bulk of the seam allowance ends.

You can now secure the three layers together for quilting using safety pins if you wish. Refer to Safety Pin Basting on page 26.

The Projects

A variety of simple, yet beautiful, projects on which to practice your utility stitching and quilting designs are showcased on the following pages.

Sampler Strippy Quilt

Quilt size: 52" x 46"

This lovely little lap quilt is a quick way to practice a variety of utility stitches and a utility quilting design in the border. The strips are easy to sew and the fabrics can be pulled from your stash.

MATERIALS AND CUTTING

Fabric
Assorted fabrics: 1½ yards
Cut 17 – 2½" wide strips
You may use Jelly Roll® strips here

Border
Print fabric: 1 yard
Cut 5 – 6½" wide strips. Remove selvages and join strips to make one continuous length. Press seams open.

Backing 3 yards
Cut two equal lengths and remove selvage. Sew the lengths together and press seams open.

Batting
60" x 54"

Binding ½ yard
Cut 6 – 2½" wide strips. Join strips diagonally to make one continuous strip. Press in half WS together along the strip's entire length.

Quilting Thread
Anchor Cotton A Broder, size 8

All fabric quantities are based on 44" usable width of fabric.
SA means seam allowance
WS means wrong side of fabric
RS means right side of fabric

METHOD

1. Lay out 17—2½" wide assorted fabric strips in a pleasing manner. Sew the strips together lengthwise. Remember to sew from opposite ends as you add each additional strip. This will help avoid distortion. Press all seams in **one** direction.

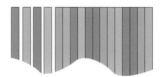

3. Square up the quilt center to approximately 42½" x 34½".

4. From the border fabric cut 2 – 6½" x 34½" strips. Sew the strips to the top and bottom of the quilt center. Press seams toward the borders.

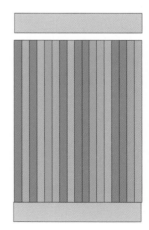

5. Measure the sides of the quilt center. Cut 2 border strips to this length. Sew to the sides of the quilt center. Press seams toward the borders.

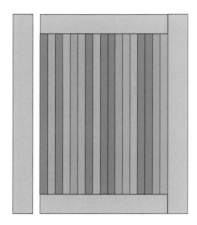

6. Layer the backing, batting and quilt top. Refer to Preparing Your Quilt on page 16 and baste the layers together using your favorite method.

Note: Do not baste along the center length of the strips, as you will be quilting here.

7. For the quilting, mark a line down the center of alternating strips. These lines will serve as a quilting guide. Choose from the quilting stitches on pages 57 - 61 and quilt along the marked lines.

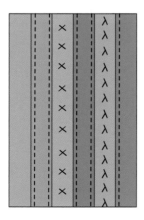

8. In the remaining rows, Big Stitch quilt ¼" away from the SA along both sides. See page 56 for Big Stitch quilting.

9. In the border, quilt ¼" away from the seam around the entire quilt. Mark the Fan design, see page 34, using the template on page 126. You may choose to quilt them freehand without any marking.

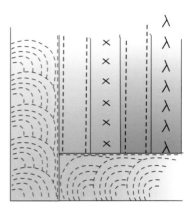

10. Bind the quilt with Square Corner binding, referring to page 74.

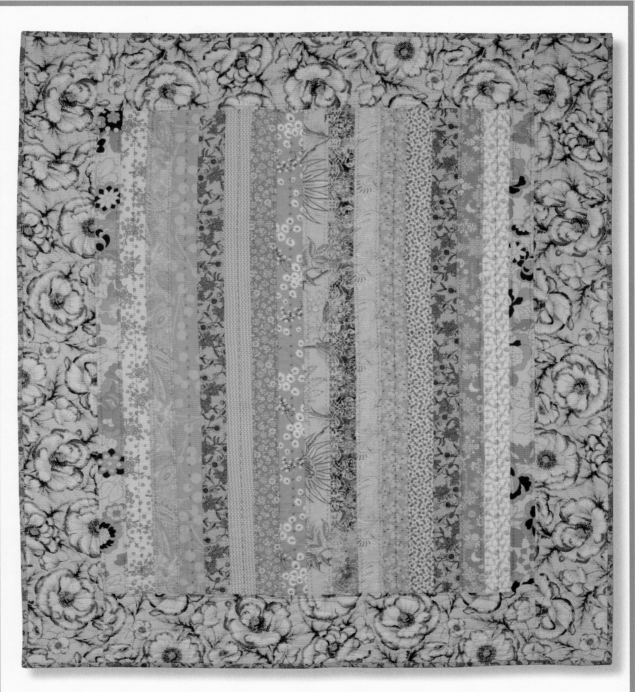

Sampler Strippy Quilt
Quilt size: 52" x 46"

Thirties Nine Patch Quilt

Quilt size: 52½" x 52½"; Block size: 17½"

Use squares from your scrap basket or your favorite charm pack to piece together this fun quilt.

MATERIALS AND CUTTING

Fabric

Assorted print fabric: 1⅝ yards

Cut 81 — 5" squares for nine-patch blocks: You may use Charm Pack squares here.

Assorted medium print fabric: ¼ yard of 9 different fabrics **OR** 9 fat quarters

From each fabric, cut 2 – 2½" x 14" strips and 2 – 2½" x 18" strips for sashing

Backing 1½ yards

Cut two equal lengths and remove the selvage. Sew the lengths together and press seams open.

Batting

62" x 62"

Binding

½ yard (if not using Turned Through Edge Finish method on page 80)

Cut 6 – 2½" wide strips. Join strips diagonally to make one continuous strip. Press in half WS together along the strip's entire length.

Quilting Thread

Valdani Pearl Cotton, size 12

All fabric quantities are based on 44" usable width of fabric.

SA means seam allowance

WS means wrong side of fabric

RS means right side of fabric

METHOD

1. Lay out 9 — 5" squares in rows as shown. Sew each row together. Press the seams of each row in alternating directions.

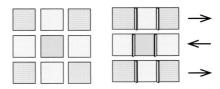

2. Sew the three rows together, pressing the seams in one direction.

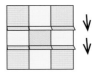

3. Sew 2 matching 2½" x 14" sashing strips to opposite sides of the block. Press seams toward the sashing strips.

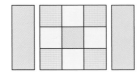

4. Sew the remaining 2 matching 2½" x 18" sashing strips to the opposite sides of the block. Press seams toward the sashing strips.

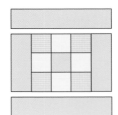

5. Repeat steps 1 – 4 to make the remaining 8 blocks.

6. Lay the blocks out in a pleasing manner. Alternate the direction of the short and long sashing strips. This will let you avoid matching up seams.

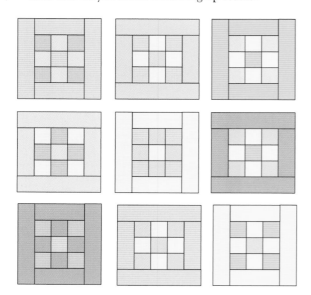

7. Sew the rows together, pressing seams toward the long sashing strips.

8. Sew the three rows together, pressing seams in one direction.

9. Lay out backing, batting and quilt top. Use the Turned Through Edge Finish method on page 80 to finish the edges of the quilt before quilting.

10. Tie the quilt at the corner of each patchwork seam. Trim the ends of the thread to equal lengths. Refer to Knots and Tying on page 62.

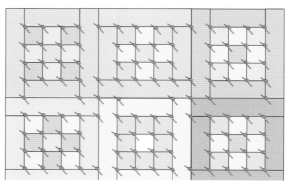

11. Sew ¼" around the outside edge of the quilt using a Big Stitch. Use the bulk of the SA as your guide.

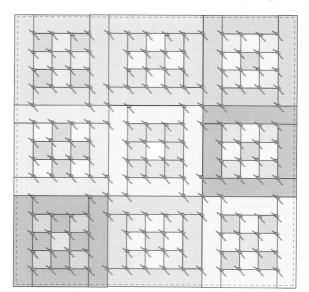

Thirties Nine Patch Quilt
Quilt size: 52½" x 52½"; Block size: 17½"

Courthouse Step Quilt

Quilt size: 72" x 72"

I love the simplicity of courthouse step quilts, but I don't always have the time to stitch a lot of blocks for a quilt. This project allows you to have the fun of stitching the block, and the ease of only needing one block for the entire quilt. I have made a scrappy version, but feel free to take a more traditional approach.

MATERIALS AND CUTTING

Fabric

Center fabric: 1 fat quarter
Cut 1 — 12½" x 12½" square

Strip A light print fabric: ¼ yard
   Cut 2 — 6½" x 12½" strips
Strip A dark print fabric: ½ yard
   Cut 2 — 6½" x 12½" strips

Strip B light print fabric: ½ yard
   Cut 2 — 6½" x 24½" strips
Strip B dark print fabric: ½ yard
   Cut 2 — 6½" x 36½" strips

Strip C light print fabric: ½ yard
   Cut 2 — 6½" x 36½" strips
Strip C dark print fabric: ¾ yard
   Cut 3 — 6½" wide strips. Join strips
   diagonally to make one continuous strip.
   Press seams open.
From this strip, cut 2 — 6½" x 48½" strips.

Strip D light print fabric: ¾ yard
   Cut 3 — 6½" wide strips. Join strips
   diagonally to make one continuous strip.
   Press seams open.
From this strip, cut 2 — 6½" x 48½" strips.
Strip D dark print fabric: ¾ yard
   Cut 3 — 6½" wide strips. Join strips
   diagonally to make one continuous strip.
   Press seams open.
From this strip, cut 2 — 6½" x 60½" strips.

Strip E light print fabric: ¾ yard
   Cut 3 — 6½" wide strips. Join strips
   diagonally to make one continuous strip.
   Press seams open.
From this strip, cut 2 — 6½" x 60½" strips.
Strip E dark print fabric: ⅞ yard
   Cut 4 — 6½" wide strips. Join strips
   diagonally to make one continuous strip.
   Press seams open.
From this strip, cut 2 — 6½" x 72½" strips.

Backing 4⅝ yards
Cut two equal lengths and remove the selvage. Sew the lengths together and press seams open.

Batting
82" x 82"

Binding ½ yard
Cut 8 — 2-½" wide strips. Join strips diagonally to make one continuous strip. Press in half WS together along the strip's entire length.

Quilting Thread
Valdani Pearl Cotton, size 12, JP11

All fabric quantities are based on 44" usable width of fabric.
SA means seam allowance
WS means wrong side of fabric
RS means right side of fabric

METHOD

1. Following the diagram sew the 2 — 6½" x 12½" strip A light print fabric strips to opposite sides of the center fabric square. Press seams away from the center.

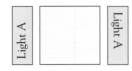

2. Sew the 2 — 6½" x 24½" strip A dark print fabric strips to the remaining two sides of the center fabric square. Press seams away from the center.

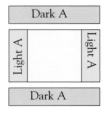 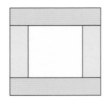

3. Continue sewing the light and dark print fabric strips around the center fabric square in the same manner until the top is complete.

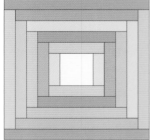

4. Layer the backing, batting and quilt top. Refer to Preparing Your Quilt on page 16 and baste the layers together using your favorite method.

5. Use the template on page 126 to mark a curve for the Fan quilting design. Begin marking in the bottom right hand corner.

Note: If you are left-handed, you will begin marking in the left hand corner.

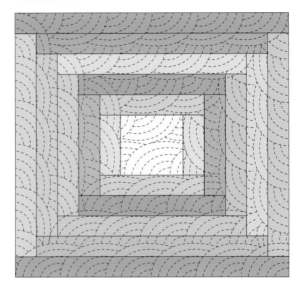

6. Continue marking the design around the outside edge of the quilt. Mark the center last. Quilt using your favorite utility quilting stitch.

7. Bind the quilt top using the Square Corner method on page 74.

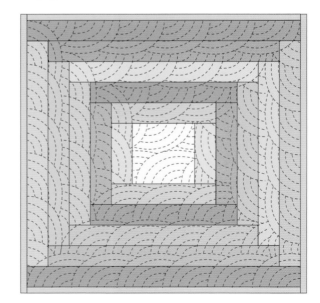

Courthouse Step Quilt
Quilt size: 72" x 72"

Square by Square Quilt

Quilt size: 67½" x 67½"

Make this simple square quilt as contemporary or traditional as you like by your fabric choice. Use charm packs or cut through your stash and use an assortment of your favorite prints.

MATERIALS AND CUTTING

Fabric

Assorted print fabric: 3⅝ yards

Cut 204 — 5" squares for quilt center and outer border

You may use Charm Pack squares here.

Light print fabric: ½ yard

Cut 2¾" wide strips. Join strips diagonally to make one continuous strip.

Cut the strips into 2 — 45½" x 2¾" and 2 — 50" x 2¾" inner border strips.

Backing 4 yards

Cut two equal lengths and remove the selvage. Sew the lengths together and press seams open.

Batting

72" x 72"

Binding

½ yard (if not using Turned Through Edge Finish method on page 80)

Cut 7 — 2½" wide strips. Join strips diagonally to make one continuous strip. Press in half WS together along the strip's entire length.

Quilting Thread

Valdani Pearl Cotton, size 12, M23

Notions

Buttons: ½" shirt buttons

All fabric quantities are based on 44" usable width of fabric.

SA means seam allowance

WS means wrong side of fabric

RS means right side of fabric

METHOD

1. Lay out 10 — 5" assorted fabric squares in a row. Stitch the blocks together. Press the seams open. Repeat to make a total of 10 rows.

2. Sew the 10 rows together to create the quilt center. Press the seams open.

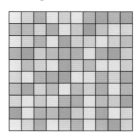

3. Sew the 2¾" x 45½" inner border strips on opposite sides of the quilt center. Press seams toward the inner borders.

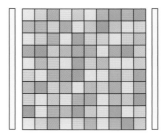

4. Sew the 2¾" x 50" inner border strips to the remaining two sides of the quilt center. Press seams toward the inner borders.

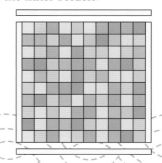

5. Lay out 22 — 5" assorted fabric squares in two rows of 11 squares. Sew the blocks together in rows and press seams open. Sew the two rows together and press seams open to make one border. Repeat to make a second border.

6. Sew a pieced border to opposite sides of the quilt top. Press seams toward the border.

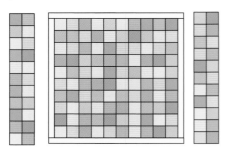

7. Lay out 30 — 5" assorted fabric squares in two rows of 15 squares. Sew the blocks together in rows and press seams open. Sew the two rows together and press seams open to make one border. Repeat to make a second border.

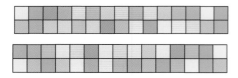

8. Sew a pieced border to the remaining sides of the quilt top, matching up the border squares. Press seams toward the border.

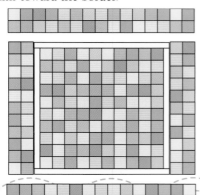

9. Lay out backing, batting and quilt top. Use the Turned Through Edge Finish method on page 80 to finish the edges of the quilt before quilting.

10. Refer to the diagram for quilting example. Buttons are attached with ties in the center of the unquilted four patch blocks.

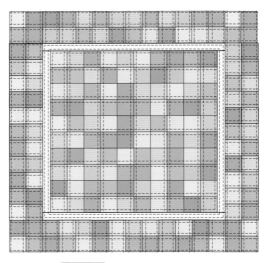

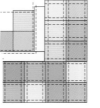 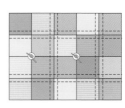

11. Quilt ¼" around the outside edge of the quilt using the bulk of the SA as your guide.

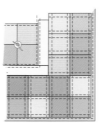

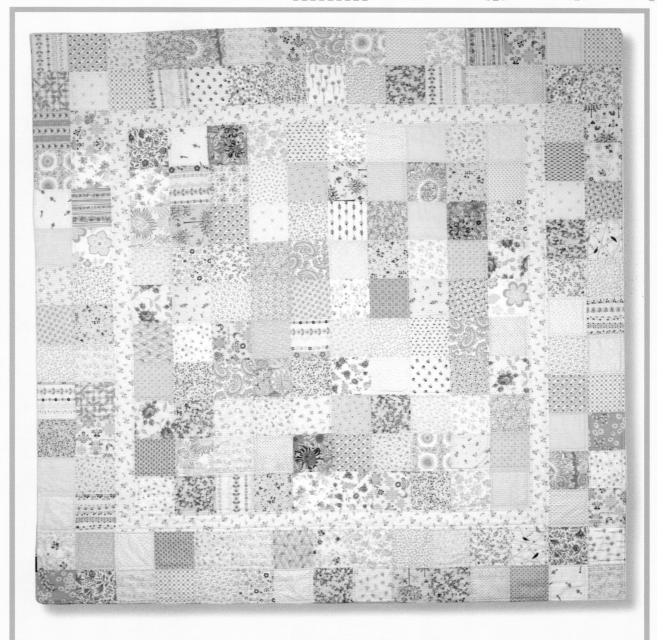

Square by Square Quilt
Quilt size: 67½" x 67½"

French Linen Quilt

Quilt size: 77" x 77"

This is a simple yet satisfying quilt to sew and quilt. The quilting on the solid fabric in the center draws the eye. The linen and cotton blend fabrics give the quilt a nice weight. It is quick and easy to quilt with larger stitches and easy flowing patterns.

MATERIALS AND CUTTING

Note: The fabric quantities for the top and binding are based on 54" wide fabric.

Fabric

Solid fabric: 1½ yards of 54" wide fabric
Trim off selvages and square the fabric to 52½" for quilt center.

Light or medium print fabric: 1⅞ yards of 44" wide fabric
Cut 5 — 13" wide strips. Remove selvages and join strips to make one continuous length. From the strip cut 2 — 13" x 52½" strips and 2 — 13" x 77½" strips for borders.

Backing 5 yards of 44" wide fabric
Cut two equal lengths and remove the selvage. Sew the lengths together and press seams open.

Batting
87" x 87"

Binding ½ yard of 54" wide fabric
Cut 6 — 2½" wide strips. Join strips diagonally to make one continuous strip. Press in half WS together along the strip's entire length.

Quilting Thread
Valdani Pearl Cotton, size 12, P4

SA means seam allowance
WS means wrong side of fabric
RS means right side of fabric

METHOD

1. Sew the 13" x 52½" border strips to opposite sides of the center fabric square. Press the seams toward the borders.

2. Stitch the 13" x 77½" border strips to the remaining sides of the center fabric square. Press the seams toward the borders.

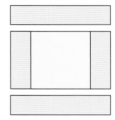

3. Layer the backing, batting and quilt top.

4. Quilt ¼" inside the seamline of the center fabric square. Stitch completely around the center fabric square.

5. Repeat the stitching outside the seamline of the center square.

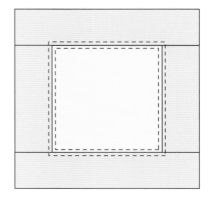

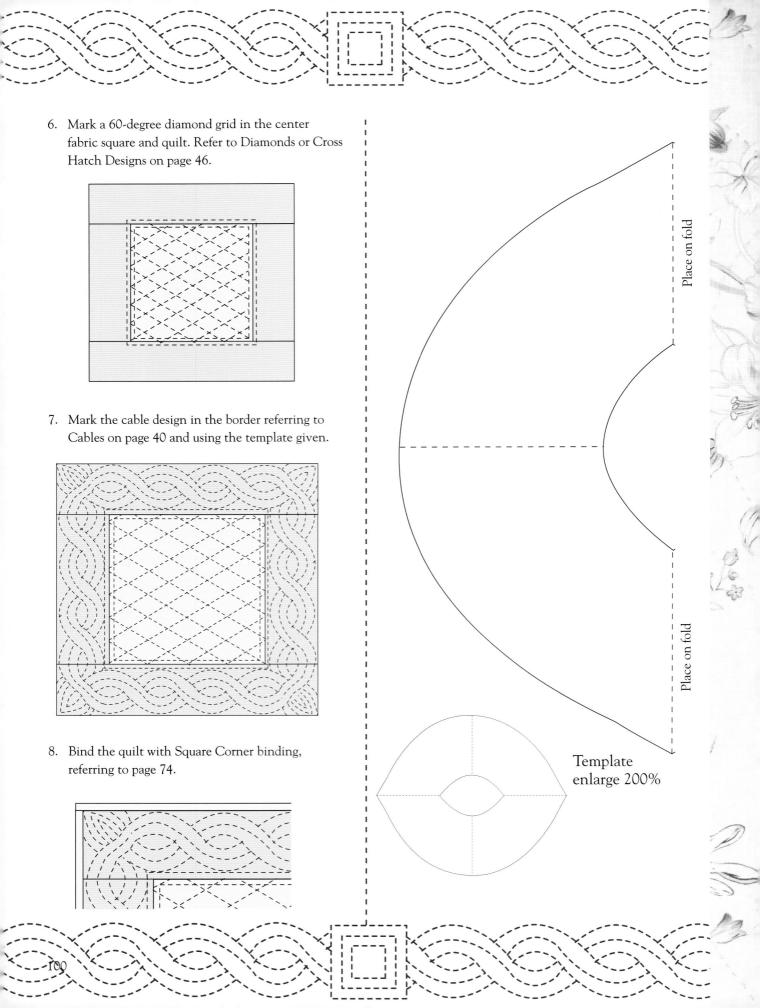

6. Mark a 60-degree diamond grid in the center fabric square and quilt. Refer to Diamonds or Cross Hatch Designs on page 46.

7. Mark the cable design in the border referring to Cables on page 40 and using the template given.

8. Bind the quilt with Square Corner binding, referring to page 74.

Place on fold

Place on fold

Template enlarge 200%

French Linen Quilt
Quilt size: 77" x 77"

Slanted Diamonds Quilt

Quilt size: 61" x 66½"

This quilt was inspired by an antique quilt dated around 1810 and seen in the book 'Quilters Album of Blocks and Borders' by Jinny Beyer. The simple method of sewing the diamonds from 5" charm squares drew me in. The cable quilting in the strips is quilting in the fast lane and the outline quilting of the diamonds needs no marking at all.

MATERIALS AND CUTTING

Fabric

Assorted medium print fabric: ⅞ yard
Cut 48 — 5" squares for diamonds
You may use Charm Pack squares.

Assorted light print fabric: ⅞ yard
Cut 48 — 5" squares for background
You may use Charm Pack squares.

Light to medium print fabric: 2 yards
Cut 4 — 9½" x 66½" strips parallel to the selvage for sashing.

Backing 4¼ yards
Cut two equal lengths and remove selvage. Sew the lengths together and press seams open.

Batting
71" x 76"

Binding ½ yard
Cut 7 — 2½" wide strips. Join strips diagonally to make one continuous strip. Press in half WS together along the strip's entire length.

Quilting Thread
Valdani Pearl Cotton, size 12, O556

All fabric quantities are based on 44" usable width of fabric.
SA means seam allowance
WS means wrong side of fabric
RS means right side of fabric

METHOD

1. Draw a diagonal line on the back of the assorted light print background squares.

2. Place a background square on an assorted medium print fabric square, RS together. Stitch ¼" away from the drawn line on either side.

3. Cut along the drawn line. Press seams toward the medium print fabric.

4. Sew the two half-square triangles from step 3 together to make a diamond. Press the seam open.

5. Repeat steps 1 – 5 to make a total of 48 diamonds.

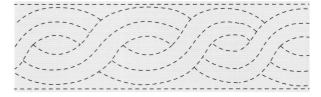

6. Lay out 16 diamond blocks. Sew the blocks together to make a 9½" x 66½" sashing strip. Press seams in one direction. Repeat to make a total of three sashing strips.

7. Sew the 9½" x 66½" sashing strips to the diamond rows, as shown. Press the seams toward the sashing strips.

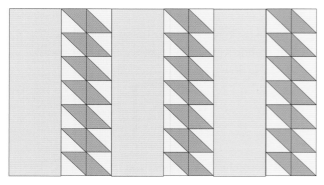

8. Layer backing, batting and quilt top. Refer to Preparing Your Quilt on page 16 and baste the layers together using your favorite method.

9. Outline quilt the diamonds. Sew ¼" around the outside edge of the quilt using a Big Stitch. Use the bulk of the SA as your guide.

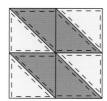

10. Use the template on page 127 to mark the cable. Quilt the central line to the cables by eye, or if you prefer mark with a dashed line.

11. Bind the quilt top using the Back Over to Front method on page 77.

Slanted Diamonds Quilt
Quilt size: 61" x 66½"

Woven Square Quilt

Quilt size: 68" x 68" Finished block: size 13"

This quilt was inspired by an idea in the book 'Slice 'Em and Dice 'Em Quilts' by Nancy Brenan Daniel. I used 5" squares to simplify the process.

MATERIALS AND CUTTING

Fabric

Assorted dark print fabric: 1 yard
Cut 64 — 5" squares

Light print fabric A: 1 yard
Cut 72 — 5" squares

Medium print fabric B: 1 yard
Cut 72 — 5" squares

Border print fabric: $1\frac{2}{3}$ yards
Cut 7 – $8\frac{1}{2}$" wide strips. Remove selvages and join strips to make one continuous length for borders. Press seams open. Border strips will be cut later.

Backing $4\frac{3}{8}$ yards
Cut two equal lengths and remove the selvage. Sew the lengths together and press seams open.

Batting
78"x 78"

Binding $\frac{1}{2}$ yard (if not using Turned Through Edge Finish method on page 80)
Cut 7 — $2\frac{1}{2}$" wide strips. Join strips diagonally to make one continuous strip. Press in half WS together along the strip's entire length.

Quilting Thread
Valdani Pearl Cotton, size 12, M32

Notions
Buttons: 16 — ¾" buttons

All fabric quantities are based on 44" usable width of fabric.
SA means seam allowance
WS means wrong side of fabric
RS means right side of fabric

METHOD

1. Lay out 1 light print A square, 4 medium print B squares and 4 assorted dark squares as shown.

2. Sew the squares together to make a Nine Patch block A. Press the seams open. Make 8 Nine Patch block A in this manner.

3. Measure $2\frac{1}{4}$" in from the seamline of the center row of each block. Cut the blocks in half in each direction and set aside.

   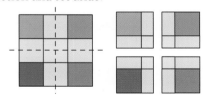

4. Lay out 1 medium print B square, 4 light print A squares and 4 assorted dark squares as shown.

5. Sew the squares together to make a Nine Patch block B. Press the seams open. Make 8 Nine Patch block B in this manner.

6. Measure 2¼" in from the seamline of the center row of each block. Cut the blocks in half in each direction and set aside.

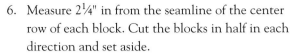

7. Using the sections from Nine Patch block A and Nine Patch block B, lay them out to create a new block. Sew the sections together and press seams open. Make 16 blocks.

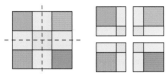

8. Lay out the 16 blocks in 4 rows of 4 blocks each. Sew the rows together, pressing the seams in each row in alternate directions. Sew the rows together, pressing the seams in the same direction.

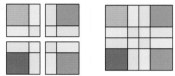

9. Measure the quilt through the center widthwise. Cut 2 border strips to this measurement. Sew the strips to opposite sides of the quilt center. Press seams toward the border.

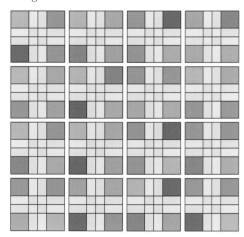

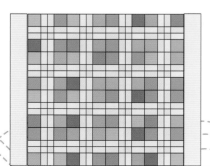

10. Measure the quilt through the center lengthwise, including the side borders just added. Cut 2 border strips to this measurement. Sew the strips to the top and bottom of the quilt center. Press seams toward the border.

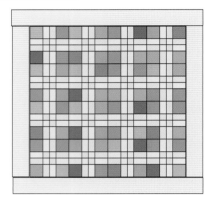

11. Layer the backing, batting and quilt top. Use the Turned Through Edge Finish method on page 80 to finish the edges of the quilt before quilting.

12. The quilt is tied at the corners of the patchwork seams. Buttons were tied in the centers of the Four Patch squares.

13. Big Stitch quilt in the border, ¼" around the outside edge of the quilt using the bulk of the SA as your guide.

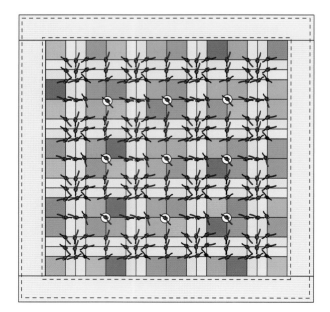

Woven Square Quilt
Quilt size: 68" x 68" Finished block: size 13"

Stretched Hexagon Quilt

Quilt size: 60½" x 72½"

This quilt was inspired by a Tumblers Quilt in the collection of quilts at the Shelburne Museum in Vermont. The original can be seen in the book 'Quilts from the Shelburne Museum'.

MATERIALS AND CUTTING

Fabric
Assorted print fabrics: ⅓ yard of 20 different prints
Tumblers will be cut in step 1

Backing 4 yards
Cut two equal lengths and remove the selvage. Sew the lengths together and press seams open.

Batting
70" x 80"

Binding
½ yard (if not using Turned Through Edge Finish method on page 80)
Cut 7 – 2½" wide strips. Join strips diagonally to make one continuous strip. Press in half WS together along the strip's entire length.

Quilting Thread
Valdani Pearl Cotton, size 12, 204, 18, O577, 775
Anchor Tapestry Wool, 9792

All fabric quantities are based on 44" usable width of fabric.
SA means seam allowance
WS means wrong side of fabric
RS means right side of fabric

METHOD

1. Cut 6½" wide strips from the assorted print fabrics. Cut a total of 228 tumbler units using the template on page 112, alternating the direction on the fabric strips as shown.

Note: Cut an even number of tumblers from each fabric. They will be paired to form the elongated hexagon. For a scrappier looking quilt, don't worry about pairing the tumblers.

2. Lay out the 228 tumblers in 12 rows with 19 tumblers in each row.

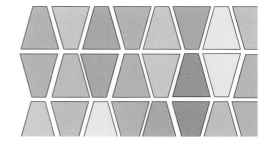

3. Sew the tumblers together in rows. Refer to the diagram to see how the edges overlap when the tumblers are sewn together. You must do this to get straight rows.

4. Press the tumbler seams on alternating rows in the same direction.

5. Sew the rows together. Press the seams open.

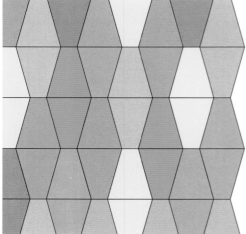

6. Layer the backing, batting and quilt top. Use the Turned Through Edge Finish method on page 80 to finish the edges of the quilt before quilting.

7. Sew ¼" around the outside edge of the quilt using a Big Stitch. Use the bulk of the SA as your guide.

8. Tie the quilt at the seam lines of the tumblers.

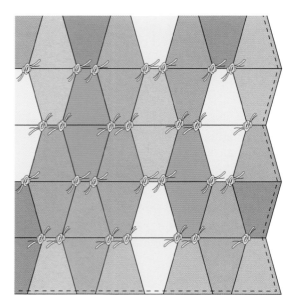

Full Size
Template

Stretched Hexagon Quilt
Quilt size: 60½" x 72½"

Australian Bush Quilt

Quilt size: 64" x 77"

In Australia, utility quilts are sometimes known as Waggas. They are named after a flour mill town in Australia. The old flour sacks were made available to families who would turn them into simple quilts in times of hardship. This quilt is inspired by a pattern from Joy Major of Australia.

MATERIALS AND CUTTING

Fabric

Assorted prints: ½ yard each of 11 different fabrics for quilt center and outer border

Medium print: ½ yard for inner border
Cut 7 — 2½" wide strips. Join strips diagonally to make one continuous strip. Press seams open.

Backing 4⅛ yards

Cut two equal lengths and remove the selvage. Sew the lengths together and press seams open.

Batting

74" x 87"

Binding ½ yard

Note: For a more cohesive look, use the same binding and inner border fabric.
Cut 7 — 2½" wide strips. Join strips diagonally to make one continuous strip. Press in half WS together along the strip's entire length.

Quilting Thread

Hillcreek Normandy Linen 30/3

All fabric quantities are based on 44" usable width of fabric.
SA means seam allowance
WS means wrong side of fabric
RS means right side of fabric

METHOD

1. Group the 11 — ½ yard assorted prints into one stack of 6 and one stack of 5, aligning the selvages. The fabrics can be in any order as this is only for the cutting.

2. Cut the fabric stacks into 3 — 12½" x 14" sections as shown in the diagram. Repeat with the second stack.

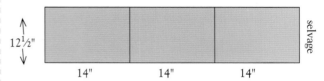

12½"

14" 14" 14"

selvage

3. Cut the fabric sections into outer border and quilt center pieces as shown. Group the same sized pieces together and label them border or quilt center. Set the border pieces aside. Set aside any extra fabric pieces for making a pieced binding.

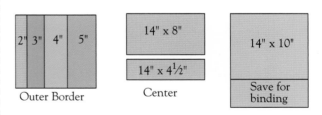

2" 3" 4" 5"

14" x 8"

14" x 4½"

14" x 10"

Save for binding

Outer Border   Center

4. Sew the short ends of the 14" x 10" pieces together to make one long strip. It does not matter which order you sew the fabrics in. Press the seams in one direction.

5. Repeat step 4 using the 14" x 8" pieces and then the 14" x 4½" pieces. You should now have three long strips of pieced fabric.

Note: Shuffle the fabrics around so each row is not the same.

6. Take one of the long strips and fold it into thirds. You may need to lay the strip on the floor as you work. Cut at the folds. Repeat this process with the two remaining long strips. You should now have nine shorter strips.

7. Arrange the nine strips in a pleasing way. You may need to rearrange the strips to ensure you get a brickwork effect with staggered seams.

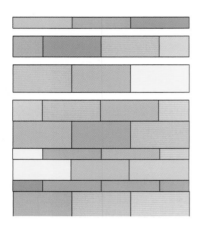

8. Sew the strips together and press the seams in one direction. Square up the sides if necessary.

9. Measure the quilt through the center widthwise. Cut 2 inner border strips to this measurement. Sew the strips to the longest sides of the quilt center. Press seams toward the inner border.

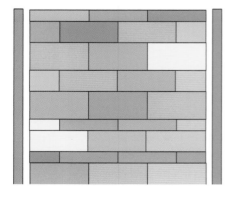

10. Measure the quilt through the center lengthwise, including the borders just added. Cut 2 inner border strips to this measurement. Sew the strips to

the top and bottom of the quilt center. Press seams toward the inner border. Set aside.

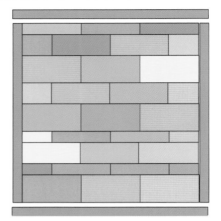

11. Sew the long edges of the outer border pieces together. Mix up the fabrics and sizes to create interest. You should now have 1 — 12½" wide border strip. Press the seams in one direction.

Note: I chain piece the fabric pieces into pairs, and then sew these pairs together. Gradually I have less and less groups to sew together.

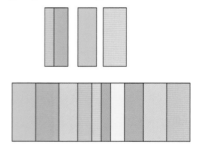

12. Carefully fold the length of the border strip in half and in half again. Using a rotary cutter and ruler cut the strip in half. Each strip will be about 6¼" wide. Sew these two pieces together to form one long border strip.

6¼"   6¼"

13. Measure the quilt through the center widthwise. Cut 2 outer border strips to this measurement. Sew the strips to the longest sides of the quilt center. Press seams toward the inner border.

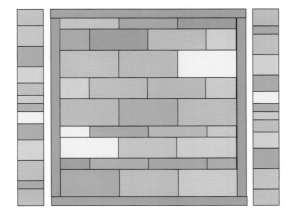

14. Measure the quilt through the center lengthwise, including the borders just added. Cut 2 outer border strips to this measurement. Sew the strips to the top and bottom of the quilt center. Press seams toward the inner border. Set aside.

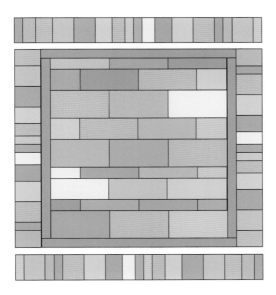

15. Layer the backing, batting and quilt top. Refer to Preparing Your Quilt on page 16 and baste the layers together using your favorite method.

16. Use the template on page 118 to mark the Teacup design in the quilt center. Remember to start in the center of the top and work out toward the frame. This will give the pattern an even edge all the way around the quilt.

17. Quilt in the ditch around the inner border on both sides. In the outer border, quilt in the ditch of each seam no matter which way it faces.

18. Bind the quilt with Square Corner binding, referring to page 74.

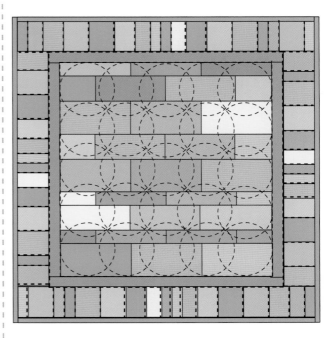

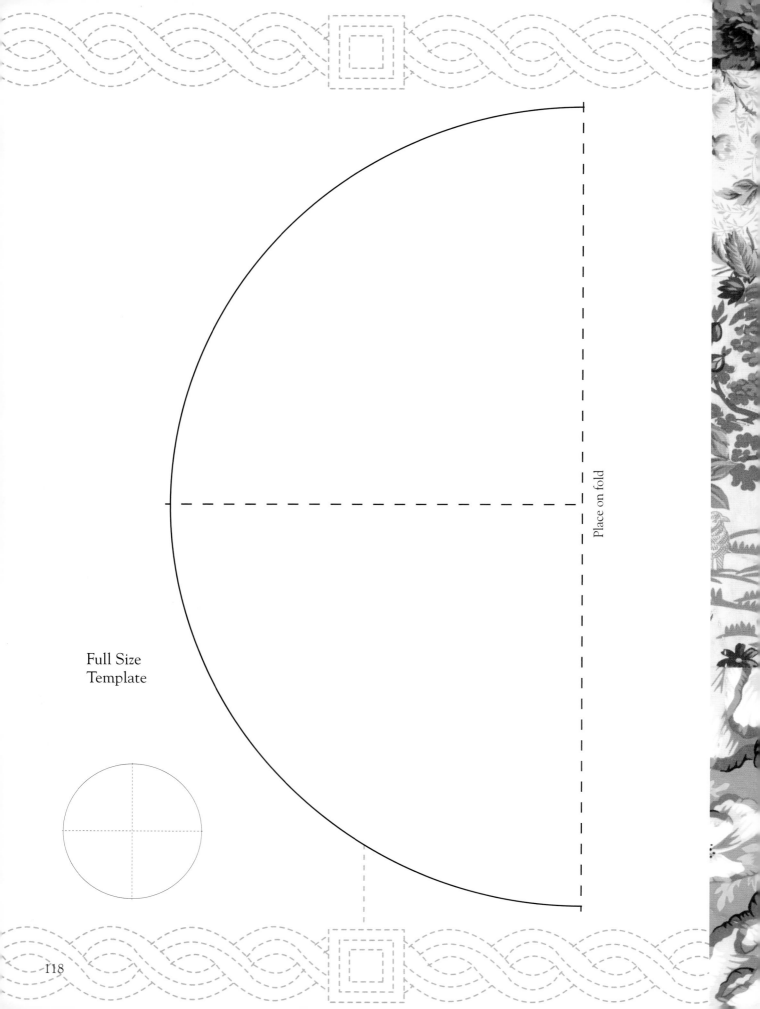

Full Size
Template

Place on fold

Australian Bush Quilt
Quilt size: 64" x 77"

Christmas Presents Quilt

Quilt size: 72" x 72" Block size: 12" x 12"

The colors in this quilt give it a seasonal feel without using any real Christmas prints. The squares are cut and re-pieced as Puss-in-the-Corner blocks making them look like presents piled high. The quilting looks like the ribbon.

MATERIALS AND CUTTING

Fabric
Assorted print fabrics: $3\frac{7}{8}$ yards
Cut 30 — $13\frac{1}{2}$" squares and
  6 — $12\frac{1}{2}$" squares

Backing $4\frac{5}{8}$ yards
Cut two equal lengths and remove the selvage. Sew the lengths together and press seams open.

Batting
82" x 82"

Binding $\frac{1}{2}$ yard
Cut 7 — $2\frac{1}{2}$" wide strips. Join strips diagonally to make one continuous strip. Press in half WS together along the strip's entire length.

Quilting Thread
Valdani Pearl Cotton, size 12, V4

All fabric quantities are based on 44" usable width of fabric.
SA means seam allowance
WS means wrong side of fabric
RS means right side of fabric

METHOD

1. Cut a $3\frac{1}{2}$" strip from each side of the $13\frac{1}{2}$" assorted print squares. Cut a $3\frac{1}{2}$" square from each end of the fabric strips. Layer the fabrics to make cutting quicker.

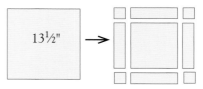

2. Shuffle the fabrics around to create different block combinations. Each block will have three fabrics.

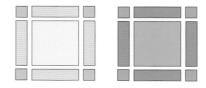

3. Sew the blocks together. Make 30 blocks.

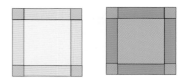

4. Lay out the 30 pieced blocks and the 6 — 12½"
   solid squares in 6 rows of 6 blocks each. Use the
   diagram for guidance.

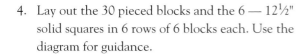

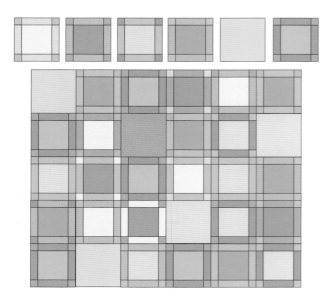

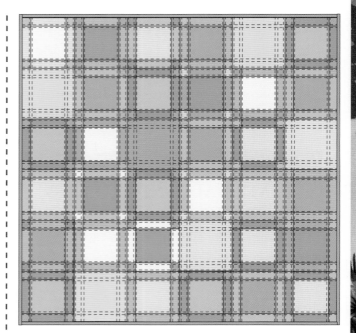

5. Sew the blocks together in rows pressing the seams
   in alternate directions on each row.

6. Sew the rows together pressing the seams in one
   direction.

7. Layer the backing, batting and quilt top together.
   Refer to Preparing Your Quilt on page 16 and baste
   the layers together using your favorite method.

8. The quilting design is stitched ¼" from the seam
   lines and continues straight across the non-pieced
   blocks.

9. Bind the quilt with Square Corner binding,
   referring to page 74.

Christmas Presents Quilt
Quilt size: 72" x 72" Block size: 12" x 12"

Coffee Cup Cozies

Project size: 11½" x 4"

Keep one of these cute coffee cup cozies handy for your favorite coffee on the run. So quick and easy to stitch and the perfect way to try out new stitches.

MATERIALS AND CUTTING

Fabric listed yields 1 coffee cup cozy

Fabric

Print fabric: ¼ yard

Cut 1 — 6½" x 13" rectangle for the front

Cut 1 — 6½" x 13" rectangle for the back

Batting

6½" x 13" rectangle

I used Insul-Bright® for its thermal qualities.

Binding

½ yard (if not using Turned Through Edge Finish method)

Cut 1— 2½" x 30" bias strip. Fold in half lengthwise, WS together, and press.

Quilting Thread:

Valdani Pearl Cotton, size 12, M360 and 18

Notions:

Button

Strong thread for loop OR large snap fastener

All fabric quantities are based on 44" usable width of fabric.

SA means seam allowance

WS means wrong side of fabric

RS means right side of fabric

METHOD

Cozy without binding

1. Using the template on page 125, lay it on the WS of the back fabric and trace around it.

2. Layer the batting and front fabric RS facing up. Lay the back fabric, WS facing up, on batting and front fabric.

3. Pin the layers together. Insert the thread loop you are using to close the cozy. Machine stitch around the drawn line. Leave an opening in the center for turning the layers through.

4. Trim the batting to the stitching line. Trim front and back layers of fabric to a scant ¼". Snip diagonally at the corners.

5. Turn the cozy RS out and slipstitch the opening closed.

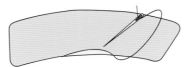

6. Quilt the layers together using a Big Stitch, alternative stitches or tying. Use the printed fabric to guide your stitching design or mark the cozy with lines.

7. Sew the button to the cozy where the mark on the template indicates.

COZY WITH BINDING

1. Using the template below, lay it on the RS of the front fabric and trace around it.

2. Layer the back fabric, batting and cozy front. Spray baste if desired.

3. Quilt the layers together using a Big Stitch, alternative stitches or tying.

4. Bind the cozy using the Machine Stitched Continuous binding method on page 71. Insert the loop closure in the binding where marked.

5. Sew the button in place on the front of the cozy.

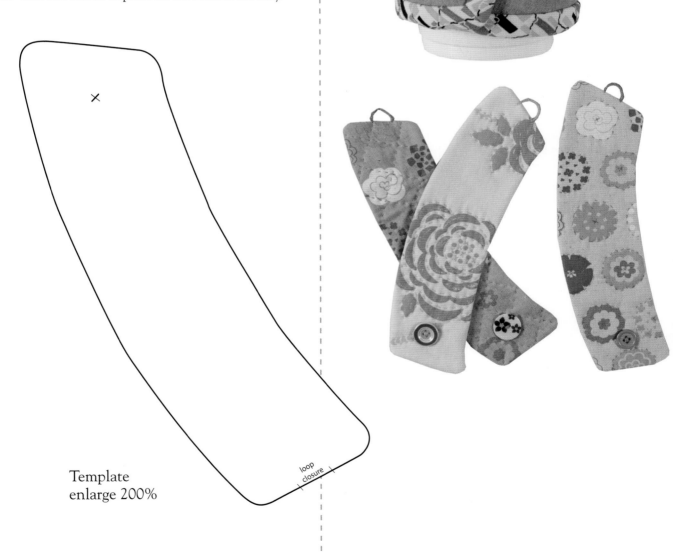

×

Template
enlarge 200%

loop
closure

Sampler Strippy Quilt
page 82

Template for
Sampler Strippy Quilt
100%

Template for
Courthouse Step Quilt
enlarge 165%

Courthouse Step Quilt
page 90

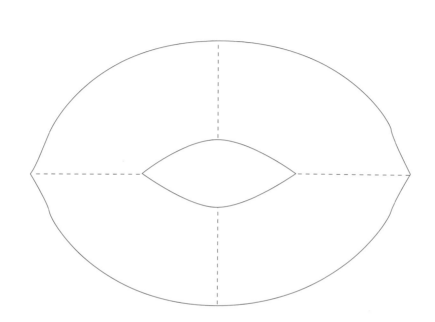

Template for
Slanted
Diamonds Quilt
enlarge 200%

Slanted Diamonds Quilt
page 102

Resources & References

Books/Articles
101 Fabulous Rotary-Cut Quilts
Judy Hopkins & Nancy J. Martin
That Patchwork Place, 1998

Big Stitch Makes a Big Impression
Jo Walters
QNM Dec 1995

Not Just Knots
Carol Johnson
QNM April 1995

Big Stitch Makes a Big Impact
Victoria Stuart
Quilting International Jan 1995

Big Stitch, a Faster Way to Hand Quilt
Jo Walters
The Quilter, no.62 Spring 1995

Quilting with Style
Gwen Marston and Joe Cunningham
AQS, 1993

Quilts from The Shelburne Museum
1996, Kokusai Art, Tokyo

Slice 'Em & Dice 'Em
Nancy Brenan Daniel
Leisure Arts 2004

The Quilter's Album of Blocks
and Borders
Jinny Beyer
EMP Publications Inc.1980, 1986

How to Improve Your Quilting Stitch
Ami Simms, 1986

Loving Stitches
Jeanna Kimball
Martingale 2003

Fine Hand Quilting
Diana Leone
Leone Publications 1986

One Line at a Time
Charlotte Warr Andersen
C&T Publishing 2009

Quilting Designs from the Past
Jenny Carr Kinney
C&T Publishing 2008

Felt
National Nonwovens
P.O.Box 150
Easthampton
MA, 01027
www.nationalnonwovens.com

Buttons
Hillcreek Designs
10159 Buena Vista Avenue
Santee, CA 92071
www.hillcreekdesigns.com

The Button Company
41 Terminus Road
Chichester West Sussex
PO19 8TX, UK
www.eternalmaker.com

Needles
www.bohin.fr

Threads
www.valdani.com

Spray Adhesive
www.Sprayandfix.com

Batting
Hobbs Heirloom
www.hancocks-paducah.com

Warm and Natural
www.hancocks-paducah.com

Antique Quilts
Cindys Antique Quilts
Cindy Rennels
PO Box 1212
Clinton, OK 73601
www.cindysantiquequilts.com

Thanks to -
My students, those I have taught
and those I have yet to meet.
Jeramy and her team at Landauer,
their support has been invaluable.
My husband Craig and son Paul,
who put up with much, but have
not starved to death yet, even
though I have quilts to stitch!